WHAT I LEARNED ABOUT
POLITICS

Inside the Rise—and Collapse—of
Nova Scotia's NDP Government

GRAHAM STEELE

NIMBUS
PUBLISHING

NIMBUS.CA

Nimbus Publishing Limited
3731 Mackintosh St, Halifax, NS B3K 5A5
(902) 455-4286 nimbus.ca

Printed and bound in Canada

NB1148

Cover photo: Courtesy of the Halifax Herald Limited
Design: John van der Woude Designs

Library and Archives Canada Cataloguing in Publication

Steele, Graham, author

What I learned about politics : inside the rise—and collapse—of Nova Scotia's

NDP government / Graham Steele.

Issued in print and electronic formats.

ISBN 978-1-77108-210-5 (pbk.).—ISBN 978-1-77108-211-2 (html).

—ISBN 978-1-77108-212-9 (mobi)

1. Steele, Graham. 2. Politicians—Nova Scotia—Biography. 3. Nova Scotia New

Democratic Party—Biography. 4. Elections—Nova Scotia. 5. Nova Scotia—

Politics and government—1999-2009. I. Title.

JL229.A8N69 2014   324.2716'072092   C2014-903180-7

C2014-903181-5

Nimbus Publishing acknowledges the financial support for its publishing activities from the Government of Canada through the Canada Book Fund (CBF) and the Canada Council for the Arts, and from the Province of Nova Scotia through Film & Creative Industries Nova Scotia. We are pleased to work in partnership with Film & Creative Industries Nova Scotia to develop and promote our creative industries for the benefit of all Nova Scotians.

For my boys, Deivan and Kiran.

Remember all those mornings I got up so early?
This is what I was writing.

Remember all those times I was away when you were
growing up? That's what I'm writing about.

And for Tilly, who put up with a lot so it could happen.

CONTENTS

Foreword vii

Preface xi

1   The Election Of 2013: "The Arse Is Right Out of 'Er"...... 1

2   Learning to Be a Politician.................................... 5

3   What Does an MLA Actually Do?................................ 23

4   Eight Years in Opposition 49

5   Election 2009: The Honeymoon Begins........................... 69

6   Inside the Dexter Government.................................. 81

7   The MLA Expense Scandal: The Honeymoon Ends 101

8   So You Want to Be Finance Minister? 107

9   The Choices We Made: Balance, Spending, Taxes 123

10   Resigning as the Minister Of Finance 141

11   Returning to Cabinet 153

12   The End 161

Appendix: The News Conference I Never Held............ 177

Acknowledgments and Further Reading 183

FOREWORD

The history teacher in front of the class of bright little faces warned the young people time and again: "There's nothing so uncertain as a dead sure thing." It was advice offered very long ago in a small town in northern New Brunswick. I was one of those "little faces" and much as I took it to heart, I didn't always heed it.

Which brings us to a few events in modern Nova Scotia politics.

Surely Vince MacLean's Liberals will easily crush an old, tired, and discredited John Buchanan-led Conservative party.

Surely health care reform in Nova Scotia will finally move forward with Dr. John Savage recruiting a brilliant, native-born, and internationally renowned physician, Dr. Ron Stewart, to formulate and enact the changes.

Surely there will be a seamless transition of power from a much-admired Tory premier, John Hamm, to his most able cabinet minister and longtime finance minister Neil LeBlanc.

And then there was the coming of the "New Jerusalem." After a long struggle, the New Democratic Party, under the leadership of a moderate, avuncular Darrell Dexter, was set to "do politics differently" in Nova Scotia. On June 9, 2009, the electorate gave the party a mandate only its most starry eyed acolytes could have dreamed of twenty years before.

"There is nothing as uncertain as a dead sure thing."

In this book Graham Steele not only explains how things came undone, but he says that on the night the party faithful celebrated victory, the seeds for their fall had already been planted.

As the finance minister for this new government, Graham's perspective on this is unique. He points out in the book that a government's real priorities are not to be found in campaign literature or in stump speeches. You must follow the money. What a government believes in, what it cares about, what it really stands for, can be understood by what it does and doesn't spend (our) money on.

Graham refers in the book to "the iron grip of the status quo." He refers here to the immense difficulty of finding new ways to operate any government. Where do you find programs and projects to defund so that new and hopefully better ones can be supported? In opposition, you might naively think you can comb through departmental budgets and find enough "loose change" to make a big difference. It just ain't so.

And new finance ministers very quickly realize that things are worse than the previous government led the citizens to believe. Such realities lead governments to look at subsidies for a Yarmouth ferry as a nice little chunk of change that could be spent better elsewhere. How did that one work out for you?

Most books about politics are written by academics, reporters, or politicians who come at the Art of the Possible from an angle different than Steele. A conventional book about this period in Nova Scotia might be expected to have more of the personal and anecdotal. It would contain more stories of the people and the strange tribal loyalties that make politics as interesting as it is in the province.

Graham does not shy from any discussion of personalities. He discusses his relationship with Premier Dexter, in all its complexities. He very clearly understands the unique duality within the party. There may have been Conservatives loyal to Neil LeBlanc and others faithful to Rodney MacDonald—that's a temporary thing. Many Liberals loyal to Jim Cowan (who lost the leadership to Vince MacLean) sat out the next election, which greatly helped John Buchanan win a third term. Most of these Liberals have gotten over that.

Graham understands and explains very well the struggle between the political pragmatists like Dexter and those longtime supporters of the party like Howard Epstein who espouse a more traditional social democratic line.

The choice not to focus on personalities and the everyday cut and thrust at the House or on the hustings gives Graham greater scope to look at areas and issues that a political scientist or political reporter might not care about as much…and could never understand without the benefit of having been an elected politician, never mind a senior cabinet minister.

Graham provides a detailed series of chapters that amount to a "how" of politics, not just here is Nova Scotia but just about anywhere else where a comparable system is in place. And trust me on this, it isn't always pretty. This is where the bit about not wanting to know how sausages and laws are made might be invoked.

One of the most interesting and insightful aspects of the book is Graham's personal journey into and out of active politics.

My grandfather was an MLA in New Brunswick for twenty-nine years. In his house, in our house, and all around the town, we talked partisan politics. The experience led to a lifelong love of the game and it inoculated me against any fever that might prompt me to seek public office.

Steele didn't come from an experience like that, and we as readers of the book are better for it. There is—and I mean this in the most positive sense—a bit of *Mr. Smith Goes to Washington* in Graham. (He even looks a little like a young James Stewart.) He went into the game for the right reasons, he tried to do the right thing(s), and he left for perfectly sound reasons about which he is both honest and forthcoming. His book is part memoir, part manual, and part cautionary tale.

Don Connolly
Information Morning
CBC Radio

PREFACE

How do you learn to be a politician?

There's no school, no textbook, no user guide.

You can learn from politicians with more experience. But all political lives end in failure—so the saying goes—so you would be learning from failures, or people on their way to becoming failures.

Besides, there's a culture of secrecy around politics. Failures don't like to admit their failings. Loyalty is rated more highly than truthtelling. A good part of politics is deal-making, and it might be hard to explain what got traded for what. Some of what politicians do or don't do can be explained only by laziness and ignorance, and who wants to admit to that?

Maybe that's why there are so few good books written by politicians about their time in politics. Apart from the culture of secrecy—which compels them to leave out all the stuff that might actually be useful to those who come after—ex-politicians are usually trying to play up their accomplishments and play down their failures. They're rewriting history. Their books are politics in another form.

So how do you learn to be a politician?

All you can do is watch and listen. That's what I did for fifteen years. And this is what I learned.

THE ELECTION OF 2013: "THE ARSE IS RIGHT OUT OF 'ER"

October 8, 2013. It's election night in Nova Scotia, and for the first time since 1998, I'm not sitting in a campaign office. Instead, I'm part of CBC TV's on-air election team in their studios on Bell Road in Halifax, along with anchors Tom Murphy and Amy Smith and veteran political reporter Paul Withers.

When Amy first called to ask me to join CBC for election-night coverage, back in the spring, I had one hesitation: I didn't want to be merely "the NDP voice" on a panel of partisans. After fifteen years in politics, I was done with partisanship. Amy assured me that wasn't what the CBC was looking for, so I said yes.

And what fun it is to see the CBC's operation from the inside. There are five rehearsals, with mock results pouring in, spread over three days. We practice two Liberal landslides, two Liberal squeakers, and an NDP squeaker. We don't practice a Conservative win of any kind.

The pre-election polls were showing a big Liberal lead. A poll released by Corporate Research Associates a few days before the election call pegged the Liberals at 41 percent, the NDP at 31 percent, and the Conservatives at 25 percent. It seemed unlikely that experienced outfits like CRA, who have always correctly called election outcomes, could be wrong about such a large Liberal lead.

Despite all the rehearsals at CBC, and despite knowing that the incumbent NDP government is almost certainly going down to defeat, my heart starts beating rapidly as we count down the last seconds to going live. This is a familiar feeling for candidates on election night. No matter how confident you are, you don't know for sure what's going to happen. The most tense time is the ten minutes between the closing of the polls and the first results. I'm a commentator now, not a candidate, but still I'm nervous. The verdict on my four years as a minister in the Darrell Dexter government—and really the verdict on all of my fifteen years in Nova Scotia politics—is bound up in the result.

As soon as the votes do start rolling in, shortly after eight o'clock, the trend is clear. The pre-election polls were right. The Nova Scotia Liberals under Stephen McNeil are heading for a comfortable majority government.

As the night wears on, the verdict on Nova Scotia's first NDP government is devastating. Cabinet ministers are going down to defeat, and for most it's not even close: John MacDonell in Hants East, Ramona Jennex in Kings South, Charlie Parker in Pictou West, Ross Landry in Pictou Centre, and Maurice Smith in Antigonish. Outstanding constituency work cannot save Clarrie MacKinnon in Pictou East, Pam Birdsall in Lunenburg, or Mat Whynott in Sackville-Beaver Bank. MLAS who normally win easily, like Dave Wilson in Sackville-Cobequid and Maureen MacDonald in Halifax Needham, find themselves in nail-biters. Frank Corbett won Cape Breton Centre in 2009 with 80 percent of the vote, the largest majority in the province. Now our deputy premier looks like he might lose. How can I describe all this? I reach for a Cape Breton expression Frank introduced to the Dexter government, and which had become a wry in-joke: "The arse is right out of 'er," I say.

Then the ultimate humiliation: the premier is defeated in his own seat. You have to go back to 1925 and a forgotten man named Ernest Armstrong to find the last time a sitting Nova Scotia premier lost his seat. Rodney MacDonald, whose tenure as premier was shorter than Darrell's, handily won his own seat in 2009 even as voters sent his Conservative government packing. So did former premier Russell MacLellan, one of only eleven survivors when his Liberal government was crushed in 1999.

The Liberals take seat after seat in the Halifax Regional Municipality, supposedly the NDP's stronghold, eventually winning twenty of twenty-four. My own constituency of Halifax Fairview no longer exists after being cut in half in the 2012 redistribution, but both the southern half (now part of Halifax Armdale) and the northern half (now part of Fairview-Clayton Park) fall to the Liberals, despite our having, in Drew Moore and Abad Khan, two smart, energetic candidates who did everything right. There is no question I would have been defeated had I been a candidate.

I watch all this calmly. My mind passes over the main events of my time in politics. Learning the political ropes, first as a caucus staffer then as an MLA. Supporting Darrell for the leadership of a divided party. Speaking out over MLA expenses and seeing Darrell angrier than I've ever seen him. Feeling responsible for a constituent going to jail. Swearing the oath as finance minister in Nova Scotia's first NDP government. Driving through a blizzard in the Annapolis Valley. Delivering four budgets. Resigning from Cabinet, for reasons known to only a few. And then returning to Cabinet in 2013 in the strangest of circumstances.

Now it's all over. My fifteen years in politics have come to—what? The first one-term government in over a hundred years. A premier defeated in his own seat.

What happened?

Let me try to explain.

LEARNING TO BE A POLITICIAN

GETTING TO KNOW NOVA SCOTIA

I arrived in Nova Scotia for the first time on a drizzly day in August 1986. I knew nobody, and there was nobody to meet me at the airport. I was going to study at Dalhousie Law School and live at King's College. A Winnipeg friend, Anne Gregory, had recommended this combination, but she had graduated and left by the time I arrived. I was alone.

I took the airport bus into town. As the bus crossed the Angus L. Macdonald Bridge over Halifax Harbour, the clouds parted and a beam of light shone on the city.

I took it as a good omen.

That first year, I hardly ventured outside a small radius around the Dalhousie campus. My only forays out of town were when Craig Scott, then a law student but now the MP for Toronto–Danforth, invited me to his family's home in Windsor for Thanksgiving and another time when I spent a sublime autumn weekend at the monastery in Antigonish County. One day I walked to Agricola Street to look for used furniture, and it seemed an adventure. It was only in my second year, when I started dating an attractive classmate from Halifax, that I got as far as Clayton Park.

I had been interested in politics for as long as I could remember. Even as a boy, I would read all the political news as I delivered the newspaper around my Winnipeg neighbourhood. I was active in the Manitoba Young Liberals and worked in Ottawa as a summer student for a federal Cabinet minister, Lloyd Axworthy, who was my Liberal MP. But when I came to Halifax for law school, I paid no attention to Nova Scotia politics. I didn't intend to stay in Nova Scotia, so what was the point?

One time in 1987 the King's College president, John Godfrey, invited me to participate in an informal chat in his sunroom with his friends George Cooper and Mary Clancy. These three political junkies got together regularly to talk politics. George had been the MP for Halifax in the short-lived Joe Clark government in 1979–80. Mary would go on to defeat Stewart McInnes in the 1988 election and remained the MP for Halifax until her own defeat in 1997. John himself was elected five times to the House of Commons as the MP for Don Valley West, a seat he held from 1993 to 2008. These were political people, and I expected to enjoy the conversation, but that evening I found their political talk impenetrable. To me, politics was about policy, but they were talking about people—and as a newcomer I didn't have a clue who they were talking about. Now, after fifteen years in politics, I know exactly why their focus was on people. Maybe someday John will reconvene the meeting with George, Mary, and me, and I will finally be able to join in. But that night I said hardly a word, and John never invited me back.

Toward the end of my last year in law school, I proposed marriage to that pretty Clayton Park classmate, and she said yes. I knew then that I would be staying in Halifax. She didn't want to move to Winnipeg, a feeling that had been frozen into place by a visit one December, and neither did I. A summer spent working at a Bay Street law firm had persuaded me that Toronto was not the place for me either. We settled into life in Halifax. I was ready to get involved with Nova Scotia politics but didn't know how.

One day we got a flyer in our mailbox from our MLA. Robert Chisholm had won a by-election just days before we moved into the constituency. The constituency had been represented for many years by Conservative premier John Buchanan, but he had left the premiership under a cloud in 1990 and taken a Senate seat. The Conservative government under Donald Cameron was not popular, and the people of Halifax Atlantic were ready for a change. Robert squeezed out a 504–vote victory over the Liberals. The Conservatives, who had held the seat for so long, were a distant third.

I responded to that flyer and dropped in on a meeting in Robert's constituency office in the South Centre Mall. That's when I joined the NDP. At the time, the Nova Scotia NDP had three seats in the legislature—Alexa McDonough and John Holm, plus Robert—so nobody could accuse me of being an opportunist. It wasn't exactly the party to join if you wanted to be a mover and a shaker. Traditionally the big law firms made sure they had both Liberals and Conservatives. When the government changed, the patronage files were put into a cart and wheeled down the corridor to a lawyer from the new governing party, and then when the government changed again, the files were wheeled back. It had never occurred to them to stock up on New Democrats.

I joined the NDP because, when I read the newspaper or listened to the radio, the NDP was the only party talking about the issues that mattered to me: poverty, housing, a clean government. I'd been a Liberal in Manitoba, but politics in Nova Scotia seemed more tribal. Political allegiances seemed to depend more on family and place than on ideas. You were Liberal or Conservative because that's what your family was. You would no more switch parties than you would switch your religion or your hockey team. I was still burning with the ideas of justice, equality, and fairness that I'd studied at Oxford and that had been reinforced at law school. I wasn't interested in tribes. The only party talking about ideas was the NDP.

I started by joining the party's policy review committee. The committee members were lovely people, but eventually it dawned on me that we were spending a great deal of time shuffling paper, with no discernible impact on our own caucus, never mind on the government. If I wanted to be where the action was, I had to be around the MLAS, or even better, I had to *be* an MLA.

The other thing I did for the NDP was more practical. A neighbourhood in Robert's constituency was suffering from groundwater problems. I volunteered to survey the neighbourhood on Robert's behalf. I knocked on all the doors, recorded all the information, and presented the results to Robert. Looking back on it now, I have no idea why an MLA was immersing himself (so to speak) in flooded basements. But it was, finally, an introduction to a different kind of politics than I'd experienced in Winnipeg or in Ottawa. It was about real problems experienced by real people where they lived. It was doorstep politics.

But then, in 1993, I took a job as in-house counsel to the Workers' Compensation Board of Nova Scotia, and I gave up any work for the NDP. The WCB had earned a reputation for being a political hot potato and a hotbed of patronage. I didn't want to give anyone a reason to question my work there. So I did nothing during the 1993 provincial election, which swept out the Conservatives. In the face of a Liberal landslide, the NDP was lucky to hold the three seats it had. Robert held Halifax Atlantic by only eighteen votes.

During my work at the WCB, I caught a few glimpses of the political life. Veteran MLA Paul MacEwan stood out because he would write detailed, passionate letters on behalf of his constituents. Often they would end up on my desk, as the WCB's lawyer, because MacEwan was making arguments the staff couldn't understand and didn't know how to answer. He rarely won his point—mainly because he would ignore or misquote any bits of the law or evidence that didn't fit his argument—but he kept on writing and writing and writing.

A more seasoned hand explained to me the realities of constituency work. Of course MacEwan wanted a favourable decision, but there was a larger objective: win or lose, he was showing his constituent that he was fighting. If the WCB's answer was favourable, the constituent would give MacEwan the credit—even if the answer would have been favourable anyway. If the WCB's answer was unfavourable, the constituent wouldn't blame MacEwan, who had gone down fighting. As a politician, MacEwan won either way.

If political longevity is success, then Paul MacEwan was the most successful provincial politician of the last forty years. The people of Cape Breton Nova elected him nine times, for thirty-three years straight, first as a New Democrat, then as an Independent, then as a Liberal. But as I watched him, I wondered what lessons I was supposed to learn.

MacEwan was the most senior MLA, along with Bill Gillis, but unlike Gillis, he was not respected by his colleagues. His speeches were one part bombast, one part reminiscence, and the rest idiosyncrasy. When he finally made it to the government benches in 1993 after twenty-three years in opposition, his own party didn't know what to do with him. John Savage named him Speaker, a role he filled controversially for three years. He was never named to the Liberal Cabinet, either by Savage or his successor, Russell MacLellan. When I started working for the NDP in 1998, MacEwan was a brooding presence on the Liberal backbenches.

I would wind up sitting beside MacEwan in the legislature, when my first term overlapped with his last. Although we were in different parties, I did literally sit beside him—he near the right rear of the Liberal seats, me at the left rear of the NDP seats, with only Wayne Gaudet between us. That's why I was one of the first people to him when he suffered a brain aneurysm at his seat in the legislature in 2002. He had already suffered an aneurysm about a year before, within days of my election to the House. After this second aneurysm, he was never the same. He did not contest the 2003 election, and Cape Breton Nova was won by Gordie Gosse of the NDP. Paul MacEwan was a passionate advocate for his constituents, and they kept voting for him, over and over. Maybe that was the only lesson a young politician needed to know.

At the same time, I saw that it was possible to stay in politics too long, past the point of good health and past the point of being taken seriously. Too many politicians stay past their best-before date, because there's nothing else for them to do. I was only just starting, but I hoped I would know when it was time to leave.

While I was at the Workers' Compensation Board I also had the chance, for the first time, to see the legislature up close. The government was sponsoring a new Workers' Compensation Act. It was the first time in eighty years that the workers' compensation law had been completely overhauled. As the board's lawyer, I had played a key role in writing the new law, and so I was taken along to meetings of the government caucus and the Cabinet. I observed how labour minister Jay Abbass shepherded the bill through the caucus, how Premier John Savage handled a Cabinet meeting, and later, how government House leader Richie Mann ran the business of the House.

Because I had spent so much time on the new law, I felt a special interest when the bill came before the legislature. I sat in the public gallery at Province House for long stretches, partly in support of Minister Abbass and partly out of curiosity. How did this place work?

I was surprised and disappointed. There were many long speeches, but no "debate" in the sense of a thoughtful exchange of views. The opposition didn't understand how workers' compensation really worked. They didn't make a serious attempt to understand what the bill was proposing. Nobody was listening anyway. The government members sat silently, waiting for the clock to run out so they could vote for the bill and move on to other business. "Nobody should watch a law or a sausage being made," Bismarck is supposed to have said (he didn't, but it's a good line), and I could see why. Lawmaking isn't an appetizing spectacle.

I left the WCB in 1997 and returned to Dalhousie Law School to do a master's degree. I was also ready to re-engage with the NDP. I made a lunch date with Robert Chisholm, who by this time was the party leader, and told him I was interested in putting my name forward as a candidate. I thought he would be keen, but he was non-committal. Maybe it was because he already had good candidates lined up where I lived and in all the surrounding constituencies. Maybe it was because I said I might contest Bill Estabrooks (who I had never met) for the nomination in Timberlea-Prospect, which would have revealed to Robert my political naivety. Whatever the reason for Robert's lack of enthusiasm, my role in the 1998 provincial election was communications for Peter Delefes's campaign in Halifax Citadel.

Peter won that election, by a handful of votes, and became the first New Democrat ever elected in the south end of Halifax. Many other New Democrats won that night, as the NDP exploded from four seats to nineteen, tying them with Russell MacLellan's Liberals. The Liberals, as the governing party, kept their grip on power. The NDP had come within a hair of forming the government.

With the big breakthrough came the need for substantially more staff at the NDP caucus office. My graduate thesis was progressing slowly, I was running out of money, and my first child was on the way. When the opportunity to be the NDP's research director came up, I jumped. I started work at the caucus office on July 6, 1998, my thirty-fourth birthday. I had finally entered the real world of politics. Not only that, but we all expected to be running the government within a year.

It took eleven.

LEARNING THE ROPES AT PROVINCE HOUSE

How do you learn politics? Real politics, not the stuff you learn in a Canadian government class in university. Electoral politics. Legislative politics. Winning politics.

The very first item I was assigned as research director was about mink farms. I was a Halifax-based lawyer with roots on the prairies. I knew nothing, absolutely nothing, about mink farms.

This is the way it is in politics: you have to know a little about a lot of different things. Name any topic, and for someone in Nova Scotia it's the most important topic in the world. For the politician, it's just the topic of the day. Yesterday it was a different topic, tomorrow it'll be something else. So you learn just enough to get by, just enough to be "political" about it. Political knowledge isn't real knowledge, but it's less work, so you go with it.

I came to the job with a good set of skills in research and writing. I knew, for example, how to use the Freedom of Information Act and how to write punchy questions for question period. I knew my way around the law, which is handy when you have only a few minutes to analyze a government bill. From the WCB I had experience in bureaucratic decision-making. I knew many of the players in the civil service and how they thought. I knew all this, but I still knew nothing about politics.

My main teacher ended up being Dan O'Connor, the leader's chief of staff. Dan is an Ontario native with Cape Breton roots. He has spent his entire adult life as a political strategist. He worked for the Manitoba NDP in the 1980s, earning praise ("remarkably able," "I was most impressed by his abilities") from former premier Howard Pawley in Pawley's recent autobiography, *Keep True: A Life in Politics*. Then he was Alexa McDonough's chief of staff, first when she was NDP leader in Halifax and then when she became federal NDP leader in 1995. He returned to Halifax a couple of years later to work as Robert Chisholm's chief of staff. He kept that position through Helen MacDonald's leadership, then Darrell Dexter's, and was eventually chief of staff in the Premier's Office of the Dexter government. He was, at all times in this story, the spider at the centre of the NDP web. The basics of opposition politics, as taught to me by Dan, were simple: Get in the news.

To get in the news, there has to be news, and not just rhetoric, in every news release. Get your facts straight, or the story will boomerang. Turn policy issues into human stories. Get non-politicians to validate what you're saying. Keep it simple. Keep the stakeholders onside. If you're going to challenge the government to do something, let it be something they can't quite accomplish. Keep the caucus happy. Above all, protect and serve the leader, who is the face and the voice of the party.

I also learned by watching the caucus. Robert was aggressive—as it turned out, too aggressive—and his attitude rubbed off on the caucus and staff. Robert was close to Darrell Dexter, who I didn't know. I learned that Darrell was a long-time strategist and organizer who was now himself in the legislature as the MLA for Dartmouth–Cole Harbour. As the NDP's health critic, he was a solid performer, though not flashy. Of course John Holm stood out, as the New Democrat with by far the most experience and the loudest voice. Maureen MacDonald and Bill Estabrooks were also very good, as were Helen MacDonald and John MacDonell. Howard Epstein excelled in the public accounts committee as it dug into Ralph Fiske's allegations about the Halifax casino. On the other end of the spectrum were a few MLAs who seemed befuddled by the whole experience.

The MacLellan government was propped up by John Hamm and his Conservatives, at least through the first year. The NDP under Robert was combative and open about its desire to see the government fall. By the spring of 1999 Hamm knew that continuing to support an unpopular government could only cause him damage. On June 17, 1999, the Liberal budget was defeated and an election was triggered.

The NDP readied itself to form the next government. How firm was this expectation? One day during the 1999 campaign I walked past Howard Epstein's office. Howard was the finance critic. He was at his desk, pen in hand, writing columns of figures on sheets of foolscap. He was writing his first budget as NDP finance minister—during an election campaign.

In the end, of course, the voters delivered a sharp rebuke to the NDP, reducing us from nineteen seats to eleven. We never got the chance to see Howard's budget. And Robert Chisholm, stung by the defeat and shamed by the late-campaign revelation of a drunk-driving conviction, resigned as leader.

HELEN MACDONALD AND THE BY-ELECTION OF 2001

At one point during the NDP's 2000 leadership convention, held in the McInnes Room at Dalhousie, I was leaning against the side wall next to Frank Corbett. On the stage were the contenders: Helen MacDonald, Kevin Deveaux, Maureen MacDonald, Dave Peters, and Hinrich Bitter-Suermann. Frank leaned over and whispered, "Which cup of poison shall I drink?"

The convention chose Helen MacDonald after three ballots. Helen was well known inside the party, but virtually unknown outside it. She had won a by-election in 1997 in Cape Breton–The Lakes following the resignation of Bernie Boudreau and then repeated the win in the breakthrough 1998 general election. But she was one of the New Democrats who went down to defeat in 1999. When she won the leadership, she had less than two years' experience as an MLA and was seatless.

Throughout her time as leader, Helen struggled to get in the news. When the legislature was in session, she camped out in the legislative library so she could be near the chamber and the media scrums. Paul MacEwan memorably referred to her as "Our Lady of the Library."

Russell MacLellan had hung on after the Liberal defeat, but eventually he resigned his Cape Breton North seat. Helen knew she had to contest the by-election and get into the House if she were going to raise her provincial profile. Cape Breton North wasn't quite her home area, but she had taught in the constituency for many years and was well known there.

Meanwhile, Eileen O'Connell, the NDP MLA for Halifax Fairview, had passed away in September 2000. The first time I worked on a Nova Scotia campaign, it was for Eileen in the 1996 by-election that followed Alexa's departure for federal politics. The riding had gone to Alexa by a modest margin in the 1993 Liberal landslide, but by 1996 the Savage Liberals were deeply unpopular and Eileen won easily.

I did some canvassing for Eileen in the by-election, and I hated it. Any negative reaction threw me off. I took it personally. Even on a winning campaign, there were enough negative responses—whether from indifference, fear, or plain old crankiness—that I dreaded going out.

And then one day, it hit me like a thunderbolt: *It's not personal—any reaction is useful information.* After that, canvassing was easy. I was no Peter Stoffer or Bill Estabrooks, the icons of NDP canvassing, but at least I'd gotten over my fear.

After Eileen's passing, the question turned to who might carry the NDP banner in the by-election. I had been mulling for a while the possibility of being a candidate. It was the right time in my life. My work as an NDP staffer would obviously not get in the way of my candidacy. If I ran and lost, the job would still be waiting for me.

I told Dan O'Connor and Pam Whelan, the senior staff of the caucus office, that I was running for the nomination. They were surprised, and unenthusiastic. They seemed mostly concerned that other candidates might criticize the caucus office for favouritism. They bent over backwards to enforce the neutrality of caucus staff. Still, a couple of staffers quietly lent a hand. Ron Sherrard and Paul Black came to my house to hear me rehearse my nomination speech. I used an ironing board in my basement as a stand-in for the podium—a modest beginning to a hoped-for career in elected politics.

There is a world of difference between being a caucus operative and being a candidate. I was grateful for some advice I got from Denis Burgess, Robert's long-serving constituency assistant: "People like it when you visit them at home." If this was the Nova Scotia way, I would do it. I set about visiting every party member in Halifax Fairview.

I won the nomination on the first ballot, against three other candidates. I had worked for it by visiting all the members, drinking a lot of tea in a lot of kitchens, but I was lucky. I signed up everyone that I or my in-laws knew in the constituency, but that still wasn't very many people. I had arrived in Nova Scotia fifteen years before, not knowing a soul, and I didn't have neighbourhood roots or school friends or family networks to turn to. In fact I didn't live in Halifax Fairview, and never did. The only thing that saved me is that two of the other candidates weren't good organizers either, and the third entered the fray too late to make a dent.

Now, after fifteen years in politics, I tell would-be nominees the simple truth of nomination meetings: it's not about issues, and it's not about speeches. It's about getting people to sign up as members, and then getting them to the hall to vote for you. If you walk into the meeting without knowing whether you've won, then you probably haven't. But I didn't know all this in January 2001. When it came to retail politics, I was an ignorant rookie.

Mercifully, John Hamm called the two by-elections only a week after my nomination, and election day was set for March 6. Mary Jane White, Eileen's sister-in-law and a very experienced organizer, agreed to manage my campaign. She could have walked away from the NDP after Eileen's passing, but she didn't. I remain very grateful to her. Sadly, she too succumbed to breast cancer only a few years after Eileen.

The campaign was an education. February was particularly cold and icy, and I was outside for most of it. I almost always canvassed by myself, which was slow and lonely and stupid, but I didn't know any better and I went at it day after day. My Liberal opponent was Jeremy Akerman, who had represented Cape Breton East through the 1970s for the NDP. I would hear that Jeremy was out canvassing, and that would force me out too.

Canadian politicians spend a lot of time going door to door, and it's one of our strengths compared to politicians in many other countries. Once you've done it, you can never forget the faces, voices, and stories of the people you've met. It grounds you. Once people realize you're not selling something, like chocolate bars or religion, they visibly relax, and are usually ready to talk.

My basic technique is to introduce myself and ask if there is anything they want me to know. That's it. That interaction on the doorstep is about them, not about me. Try to open the tap, then listen. Nice and easy, no hard politicking. Not everybody does it that way, but that's what works for me.

Halifax Fairview is an urban, residential community, with lots of variety packed into a small space. I met rich and poor, young and old, healthy and sick, long-established and new immigrant, friendly and obnoxious. I was warned away from the guy with a reputation for a violent temper, kept away from the dogs (who were mostly inside anyway, since it was February), and on the worst weather days, worked the apartment buildings. Among the many encounters during that first campaign, I remember the woman struggling to care for her husband with advancing Alzheimer's; the man who would never support the NDP because a union hadn't supported his father fifty years before; the senior whose advice was simply "remember the seniors"; and the woman who ran after me down the street and became one of my best campaign workers.

I learned how beloved a good politician like Alexa McDonough can be. When I knocked on doors with her, my constituents were far more excited to see her than to meet me. I was touched, too, by the people who told me about Alexa's father, Lloyd Shaw. I am very sorry that I never met Lloyd, because he must have been something special. Decades after he had canvassed the same streets, people in Fairview were still talking about him.

I was also introduced to voter cynicism. One common refrain I heard was "You're all the same." Another was "What difference does it make if I vote or not?" The most extreme example of cynicism was the woman who opened her door, pointed her finger at me and said, "You're all liars, and I'm not going to vote for any of you" and slammed the door.

It's hard to get used to being seen as just another lying politician. This early encounter on the doorstep, before I'd done anything and before anyone knew who I was, was a warning: no politician starts with a clean slate.

Election day was one of the worst days of the winter. A strong, cold wind blew sleet sideways all day. I knocked on one supporter's door to offer a ride to the polls. My face was crusted with ice. She looked out at the wind and the sleet, and at me, and flat-out refused to leave her home. I pleaded, but she shook her head and said, "There's *no way* I'm going out in this."

Voter turnout that day was under 29 percent, a record low for a provincial by-election. When historians are puzzling over the low turnout, I hope they don't come up with any fancy theories. The reason is simple: the weather was awful. The good news is that of the people who did turn out, 58 percent voted for me.

I was the new MLA for Halifax Fairview.

Over in Cape Breton North, which was also holding a by-election that day and where the weather was much better, voter turnout was a healthy 68 percent. The bad news was that our leader, Helen MacDonald, came a disappointing third in a contest won by Cecil Clarke, later a Cabinet minister in the Hamm and MacDonald governments and now the mayor of the Cape Breton Regional Municipality.

Despite the loss, Helen was determined to carry on as leader. This caused concern among some of my caucus colleagues. I had little involvement in the drama that ensued. It didn't play out the way people thought. There was no full caucus meeting where her resignation was demanded. There was no letter from caucus members asking her to step down. There was only a phone call from Frank Corbett to John Hugh Edwards, who had been Helen's leadership campaign manager and who remained in her inner circle. Frank was loyal to Helen but told John Hugh that six caucus members wanted to meet with her. A couple of days later, on April 24, 2001, without any meeting actually taking place, Helen resigned.

I was not part of the group that wanted to meet with Helen, but I do not blame them for being concerned. Helen had struggled with her political profile. Her departure was close to inevitable after the by-election loss. The request for a meeting to discuss her future should have been expected.

In the midst of this turmoil, I heard John MacDonell and Darrell Dexter discuss whether Helen had what it took to lead us. John remarked that Helen's image was "out of date." Darrell's memorable reply was "loyalty is never out of date." I noted that Darrell didn't disagree with John. He simply put a higher value on loyalty.

I like loyalty too, but it has limits. I couldn't see how Helen would appeal to the electorate. I'd just been elected under her leadership, but my election was due to the groundwork in the constituency by Alexa McDonough, Robert Chisholm, and Eileen O'Connell, coupled with local dislike for a Conservative government well past its honeymoon and a leaderless Liberal party that people had not yet forgiven for the turmoil of the Savage years. Helen had been a non-factor for me in the by-election.

There was no rush to push Helen out. We were facing a majority government. We were two years away from an election. She had won the leadership less than a year before. There were good reasons why party members had picked her over Kevin and Maureen. She had solid regional support from Cape Breton members. She seemed more likely than Kevin or Maureen to expand the party's base outside Halifax. But sometimes what makes sense on the convention floor, when people are voting their second or third choice, doesn't make sense to the general public—ask Joe Clark, Stockwell Day, Stéphane Dion, Russell MacLellan, Rodney MacDonald. That's where we were with Helen.

I went on CBC TV that evening as a Helen supporter. I shared the interview with Kevin Deveaux, who argued that Helen's departure was unfortunate but necessary. I was a rookie MLA, only weeks into the job, and here was my party tearing itself up over leadership. It was not what I wanted my first in-studio television interview to be about. Later I went to Helen's apartment at the Carleton Hotel, a couple of blocks uphill from the legislature. A few supporters were gathered to commiserate. Helen had seen my CBC interview and gave me a hug.

Helen MacDonald is a thoroughly pleasant, deeply decent person. Some said she was too schoolmarmish, too naive, not electable. Maybe that's so, but why shouldn't someone like her be able to succeed in politics? Now, more than a decade after her brief leadership, she is barely remembered. All political careers end in failure, but it is your own party that will really break your heart. That was certainly true in Helen MacDonald's case. After that gathering in her apartment, I rarely saw her again.

Helen's departure created considerable bitterness in the party. My colleagues who had wanted to discuss Helen's future with her were reasonable people who had reasonable concerns following the by-election loss. But Helen's supporters were not in an understanding mood. At the next party convention there was a movement to censure the six caucus members who had wanted to meet with Helen. There was a heated debate behind closed doors. If Helen had chosen to stay and fight, the party could have faced an ugly war. But she was already gone, and her supporters knew they had to move on.

After Helen's resignation, Darrell Dexter started making the rounds within caucus, looking for support to be named as interim leader. The decision on interim leadership belonged to the party's council, but the caucus's recommendation would carry considerable weight.

There are, within the Nova Scotia NDP, two broad factions. They overlap, and individuals slide from one to the other, but there are two. One is moderate, pragmatic, centrist. The other is more contrarian, more ideological, less accommodating. Faction 1 sees Faction 2 as inflexible, pushy troublemakers. Faction 2 sees Faction 1 as weak, liberal sellouts. Faction 1 is larger and almost always carries the day at party meetings, but Faction 2 is louder.

Darrell Dexter is the incarnation of the first faction.

Among the names being mentioned in the media as possible leadership contenders was my own. I was a fresh face, I could make a speech, and my work as research director gave me a superficial command of all the issues of the day, plus familiarity with provincial journalists. My lack of political experience should have immediately eliminated me as a contender, but it didn't. I never intended to run for the leadership, but I enjoyed the attention and was happy to string it along for a little while.

One night, Darrell drove me home from the legislature, for the first and only time. We both knew he wanted to talk about the leadership. We chit-chatted during the fifteen-minute drive. When we got to my driveway, we got down to the real business. I told him I would not be a contender. We talked about the two factions in the party, and I told him we were in the same faction. I would support him for the leadership. I wouldn't say that I was excited about Darrell's leadership bid. He was not charismatic or bold, but rather safe and solid, which are harder qualities to sell to the public. But he was my kind of New Democrat, and I definitely didn't want the other faction to take control of the party.

The other faction coalesced around John MacDonell, which was odd, because he wasn't one of its natural members. Maureen and Kevin opted not to enter the race, even though it was such a short time after their 2000 leadership runs. Both supported John. Howard Epstein, who is the incarnation of the contrarian faction, also supported John.

Darrell easily won the leadership convention, held in the McNally Auditorium at Saint Mary's University. For the first time ever, the leadership was decided by a vote of the full membership. The convention was low-key because almost all the votes were already in the box when it started. Darrell's margin of victory was roughly 2:1, which is a good approximation of the two factions' strength.

And so began the slow, patient build that culminated in the election victory of 2009.

3

WHAT DOES AN MLA ACTUALLY DO?

So I was an MLA—a Member of the Legislative Assembly.

How do you learn to be an MLA?

An MLA has no job description. There's no training. A veteran MLA or an experienced staffer may offer advice, but there's no systematic effort to orient the new MLA. Besides, what works for one MLA may not work for another. MLAs bring very different skill sets and experiences to the job. Each constituency is in some way unique, so each MLA is left to create his or her own version of what it means to be an MLA. Many struggle, but few admit it, because they don't want to be thought weak.

There's also no supervision. MLAs spend time in their constituencies, but nobody tracks them. They travel back and forth between constituency and downtown Halifax, and around the constituency. They operate out of their homes, their cars, and their constituency offices. They have one or two employees. A constituency assistant isn't about to reveal what the MLA gets up to, because his or her paycheque depends on discretion. Besides, once MLAs leave the office, assistants don't always know where they are or what they're doing.

When the legislature is sitting, you can see your MLA in his or her seat, but there's no public record of attendance and no systematic recording of votes. Unless you watch from the public gallery every day, there's no way of knowing if your MLA is there or for how long. Even when they're in the building, most of them are in and out, anywhere but in their seat. And when the legislature is done, the fifty-one MLAs head back to their constituencies, and any one of them doesn't know what the other fifty get up to.

LEGISLATIVE WORK

The Way It's Supposed to Work

There is one thing that only an MLA can do: sit in the House of Assembly and vote on laws and budgets. Nobody else is allowed into the chamber. Nobody else can speak. Nobody else can vote. No substitutes are allowed.

So legislative work—enacting laws and adopting budgets—is the core of the MLA's job.

Province House is where the legislative work happens. It was built two hundred years ago to house Nova Scotia's legislature, and it has served that purpose continuously ever since. It's Canada's oldest legislature. It's a pre-Victorian gem, sitting in the heart of downtown Halifax, between the harbour and Citadel Hill. A wrought-iron fence encloses the small public park in which it sits. The famous statue of Joseph Howe, still Nova Scotia's most recognized politician, even a century and a half after his death, stands in the southern yard. The northern yard, now a paved parking lot, features an equally striking but less well-known memorial to the Boer War.

The second floor of Province House is where the action is. At the southern end is the Red Room, the most beautiful room in Nova Scotia, the home of the now-abolished upper house. In the middle of the second floor is the Legislative Library, with its winding staircase and gallery. When it was still a courtroom, this is where Joseph Howe gave his stirring defence to a charge of criminal libel. His acquittal paved the way for freedom of the press in Canada.

At the northern end of the second floor is the legislative chamber, which hosts fifty-one elected members for three months out of every year.[1] The norm these days is for the House to sit for two months in the spring, typically from late March to the Victoria Day long weekend, mostly to consider the annual budget. It also sits for a month in the fall, typically starting in late October. Every session is open to the public, is broadcast on television, and has a verbatim transcript.

Here's how the legislature is supposed to work.

New laws can be proposed in both the spring and fall sittings. Anyone can propose a new law in the form of a "bill." The bill can do something new, or it can amend or repeal an existing law.

In order to become a law, a bill must go through three stages. These are called "readings," but the bill is not literally read aloud. The introduction of the bill is "first reading." The bill's sponsor stands and reads the title. The bill is then copied and distributed to all members. Approval in principle is "second reading." That's when most of the debate occurs. During second reading debate, any MLA can stand to argue for or against the bill. If a bill passes second reading, it moves on to a committee (the Law Amendments Committee) that hears from the public. From there, it passes back to the House for examination in detail (Committee of the Whole House). Final approval is "third reading." And once a bill passes third reading, it becomes law when the Lieutenant-Governor signs it (Royal Assent). It enters into force on Royal Assent, unless the bill specifies a different date or permits the government to choose a date.

Apart from passing new laws, the principal business of the legislature is to approve the annual budget. In many ways, this is the true

---

1   Throughout my time in the House (2001–2013) there were fifty-two seats. After redistribution in 2012, which took effect for the 2013 election, there are fifty-one seats. For the sake of consistency, I will use the number fifty-one throughout this book.

heart of democratic government. The formation of British-style government was motivated by the desire to control the raising of money through taxation and to control the purposes for which tax money was spent. That is why only the government is permitted to propose revenue or spending measures. The budget's importance is underlined by the rule that a government must resign if it loses a budget vote.

The budget is usually proposed in the spring sitting, which is why the spring sitting is longer than the fall sitting. The budget debate ("Estimates") has a special set of procedures. The budget is divided into two parts, and each part is discussed for forty hours. This eighty hours of budget debate is spread over a minimum of ten sitting days.

That's it, simple and clear. Fifty-one elected representatives get together in a beautiful old building in downtown Halifax to debate bills and budgets. After the debate, they vote. The majority wins.

This is responsible government in action.

Except the Nova Scotia legislature doesn't really work that way. It is, in fact, a parody of democracy.

The Way It Really Works

The first time I stood in the House to give a speech, on March 23, 2001, it was a special moment for me. Few people stand for public office, and fewer are elected. I had picked up some insights on the campaign trail that I wanted to share with my new colleagues in the House.

And so I was startled to realize, as I gave my maiden speech, that no one in the room, absolutely no one, was listening. In any other gathering of grown-ups, this would be shockingly bad manners. About fifteen minutes into my speech, I stopped, and you can almost hear the surprise in my voice:

> MR. STEELE: ...Just because the government has decided
> to build a new school to replace a sick, old school doesn't

mean that is the end of the issue. One of the most impor-
tant issues in what I will call Fairview proper, the Fairview
portion of Halifax Fairview, is what is going to happen to
the old school site.

Mr. Speaker, I paused there for a moment because as a
new member, I wasn't sure if this level of noise was normal
in the House, perhaps it is. It is something that I would
like the members on the other side to hear...

But in the Nova Scotia legislature, ignoring the person speaking, and a general background clamour, *is* normal. Here's Speaker Murray Scott in reply:

MR. SPEAKER: The honourable member has the floor.
Just to answer your question, it is probably fairly quiet for
what it can be sometimes. It is probably fairly quiet for
what it will be in the future. The honourable member for
Halifax Fairview has the floor.

MR. STEELE: I know the members are being kind enough
not to actually heckle me while I am talking. I know that
will change in due course. I know that will change. I would
like the members on that side of the House to hear, because
the most important public policy issue in the Fairview part
of Halifax Fairview remains the Halifax West High School.

The ideal is that our elected representatives listen to each other carefully and make up their minds accordingly. The reality is that our MLAS mostly ignore each other: they chat with their neighbours, read the newspaper or a book, fill out the crossword, and in the fall sitting, sign Christmas cards. As technology has advanced, the in-House habits of our MLAS have changed too: now they watch movies, listen to music, and incessantly email and text. Look down from the public gallery, and you'll see that most MLAS are peering at their smart phones or tapping on a laptop computer.

When our MLAS do pay attention to what someone opposite is saying, it is usually to heckle, interrupt, even insult. The last thing on their minds is mature consideration of someone's argument, which is fitting, because the speaker is rarely making an argument worthy of mature consideration. The MLAS who stand to speak rarely do any research and usually read a script written by staff. They routinely speak off-topic, misrepresent facts, distort what others have said, and talk mostly about themselves and their constituency.

Of course the legislature has its moments of lucidity. Occasionally the place can stand up straight and be everything it's supposed to be. These tend to be special occasions, when the tone is formal and everyone knows misbehaviour will jar. On some other occasions, an individual MLA will speak with real insight and real emotion. The House becomes still and attentive, because the members know they're hearing the real deal. But these moments are rare. More importantly, they don't persuade anyone to vote differently than they otherwise would have.

I have never worked in a place as thoroughly dysfunctional as the Nova Scotia legislature. Fifty-one grown-ups act in ways that, if repeated in their private lives, would end their personal relationships, and if repeated in other workplaces, would get them fired. Visitors to the gallery often go away shaking their heads in bewilderment, just as I had when I observed the passage of the Workers' Compensation Act. Groups of schoolchildren watch grown-ups act in ways that they, the children, have been repeatedly told not to act.

Why does this happen? How did we get to this point? Does it have to be this way?

There should be no mystery here: MLAS are responding in normal, predictable ways to their environment. There are three environmental forces at work: MLAS' background and experience do not equip them for legislative work, all substantial decisions on bills and budgets are made elsewhere, and party discipline drives all real debate behind closed doors. That's why the House is a parody of democracy.

MLAS' BACKGROUND AND EXPERIENCE DO NOT EQUIP THEM FOR LEGISLATIVE WORK

Our legislature is full of pleasant, gregarious, community-minded people who are fairly clueless when it comes to reading, understanding, and debating laws and budgets. If they have those skills, it's a lucky coincidence.

To understand a bill properly, you first have to understand the issue that the sponsor of the bill is getting at. This is hard enough, because of the bewildering variety of topics for which the provincial government is responsible.

Even if an MLA understands the issue behind a bill, the next barrier is the language of the bill. Bills are legal documents, and they're written in a style that's like a foreign language, which new MLAS do not know and which many veteran MLAS never learn. The House has a staff of lawyers who specialize in the arcane language and rules of legislation. Nobody else is permitted to write a bill, or even an amendment.

So unless a bill is short and the subject-matter readily understandable, most MLAS don't read the bills. Exactly the same can be said of financial statements, which are the other half of the legislature's bread and butter. The provincial budget consists of a stack of documents. No MLA ever reads it all. Even if an MLA did read it all, he or she would not really understand what's going on inside a department. The departmental business plans—which by themselves comprise another thick volume—should help make sense of the numbers, but they're written with deliberate blandness. An MLA has to be sharp and experienced to read between the lines and see what's actually going on. Most don't even try.

Why should we be surprised? The way that parties choose candidates isn't designed to find good legislators. Sometimes there's a contested nomination meeting, but those are all about signing people up and getting them to the meeting hall. Sometimes the parties will seek out a candidate who fits a profile likely to attract votes or someone who is well known in the community. Sometimes the parties have trouble finding a candidate and will take anybody who's willing and presentable. In none of these scenarios does ability as a legislator enter into the calculation. The only ability the parties really care about is electability.

Voters have a role in this too. Typically they're voting primarily for a party or a leader, or against a party or a leader. They're not thinking about who, among the local candidates, is most likely to be a skilled legislator any more than they're thinking about the colour of the candidates' hair. The combined result of the nomination and election processes is an almost comic mismatch between the skills required to be a good legislator and the skills that our MLAS actually bring to the House.

MLAS have adopted a variety of coping strategies to deal with their low level of legal and financial literacy. Among them:

- On the opposition side, they divide up the work among themselves into "critic" areas, then they defer to their party's critic. On the government side, there is complete deference to the responsible minister.
- They rely greatly on caucus staff and read whatever staff write for them. Most questions in question period or in committee, and many speeches at other times, are read from a script prepared by staff.
- They look for political advantage rather than a grasp of policy details. Essentially, both sides fight over public reaction to the bill or budget and how they can manipulate it, rather than on the substance.

- They focus on their own constituency, which is the one subject on which they are the acknowledged expert.

Nova Scotia's MLAS could raise their level of legal and financial literacy, but they don't want to. For one thing, they tend to see themselves as achievers who are bringing life experience and common sense to the business of government. They don't readily accept their need to upgrade their skills—they were good enough to be elected, weren't they? It is very common for new politicians to attribute their election to their personal qualities. Few will acknowledge they are virtual unknowns in their constituency and that most voters were voting for the leader or the party.

The other reason why MLAS resist training is that, of all the things in which they could invest their time, the political return on building their legislative skills is low. They resist not because they are stupid and like it that way, but quite the opposite—they resist because they are smart maximizers of their time. The greatest political return on their time is in the constituency, working toward re-election, so that's where they want to spend their time.

ALL SUBSTANTIAL DECISIONS ON BILLS AND BUDGETS ARE MADE ELSEWHERE

The truth is that Province House is not the place from which Nova Scotia is governed. The real decision-making about everything—health, education, support for the poor and disabled, justice, transportation—happens behind closed doors in office buildings scattered around downtown Halifax.

By the time a bill or a budget is tabled in the House, the government is rarely open to any amendment. The content has already been decided in the Premier's Office or in a minister's office or in the government caucus office. Politically, they cannot allow any amendment that would allow the opposition to take credit, which is just as well, because the opposition rarely understands an issue well enough to propose any sensible amendments. By the time the opposition MLAs get to the House, they too have already staked out a political position. The tactics have been decided in advance by the House leaders. Speeches are made, but nobody is open to persuasion. Members' bodies are present at Province House, but their heads and their hearts are back in the constituency.

This phenomenon reached its logical conclusion in the spring sitting of 2013, when Manning MacDonald, the veteran Liberal MLA for Cape Breton South, didn't bother to show up at all. He went on vacation to Florida instead. His defence, when he was asked to justify his absence, was revealing. As he told the *Chronicle-Herald*, "The constituents are not paying me to be in the House, they're paying me to do my constituency work. I was in touch with them every single day I was down there. I checked my messages every day and I called everybody that's interested in getting something done—every single day. And when I'm sitting in the House, I'm there watching the NDP and a majority government—there's nothing I can do about anything that happens in there, but there's a lot I can do in my constituency."

An MLA was finally admitting that he saw no value in attending the legislature at all. Manning knew that an individual MLA has zero impact on either bills or budgets, especially in the face of a majority government. Manning knew that constituency work is the only work that constituents value. The MLA doesn't even need to be in the constituency. Constituency work can be done from anywhere with a phone and an Internet connection, like Florida. These things are true—and every MLA knows it—but it took someone with Manning's bravado to say them out loud.

In politics, regrettably, the undecorated truth is usually unwelcome. The backlash to Manning's remarks was immediate. He resigned shortly afterwards, in order to save himself and his leader further embarrassment. He hadn't intended to re-offer anyway, and the election was imminent.

Manning MacDonald had a long career in elected office, first as mayor of Sydney for fifteen years and then as an MLA for twenty years. Along with Paul MacEwan, he was the most successful Nova Scotia provincial politician of his generation, if success is measured in longevity. Both built their political careers on a tight, personal connection to their constituents. When Manning resigned, he was the longest-serving MLA currently sitting in the legislature, along with Clare's Wayne Gaudet. It is unfortunate his career had to end on such a sour note—especially because he was only speaking the truth.

PARTY DISCIPLINE DRIVES ALL REAL DEBATE BEHIND CLOSED DOORS

Politics is a team sport. You have a team. There are other teams who would like to see you fall flat on your face. At the next election they are going to try to take your job away. So you want to get the upper hand over the other teams. Once you have the upper hand, you want to keep it. You want to win. And you can't win on your own.

Individual members discipline themselves, and each other, in order to maintain a facade of party unity. The party leadership doesn't need to say "you must vote this way, whether you like it or not, because we say so." They're capable of it—and when all else fails they will indeed threaten and cajole—but usually it's not necessary.

Veteran MLAs and staffers warn you that your opponents and the media will jump all over you if they see any daylight between you and someone else in your party. I saw it a few times when Mark Parent or Howard Epstein would muse aloud about not supporting something their caucus was doing. It's an easy story. The leaders always get dragged into it, and they don't like it. Any difference of opinion within the caucus is taken as a challenge to the leader's ability and authority.

Any benefit from expressing yourself honestly is outweighed by damage to the team.

If you do break from your team, punishment follows. Even in opposition, there are caucus posts, committee positions, and travel, all in the control of the leader and caucus, and all of which can be denied to someone who is not toeing the line. In government, there are all of these things, plus Cabinet positions and all kinds of legislative, budgetary, and constituency favours. Ask Brooke Taylor, who paid for questioning John Hamm's leadership by being excluded from Hamm's Cabinet, despite his seniority. Ask Howard Epstein, who was excluded from the Dexter Cabinet, despite *his* seniority. The punishment can go on for years. Politicians have long memories.

In my fifteen years in politics, I can remember only a handful of times when an MLA was willing to stand up and vote differently than the rest of his caucus. There was Jon Carey and Cecil O'Donnell voting against the extension of common-law benefits to same-sex couples in 2001. There was Cecil O'Donnell voting against a back-to-work law for health care workers, also in 2001. There was Kevin Deveaux voting for a tax break for the Dartmouth refinery in 2004. And then there was me, breaking with my party in 2005 over expenses.

SUMMING UP THE LEGISLATIVE WORK

Manning MacDonald told me once, shortly after being thrown out of the House for bad behaviour, that he did it deliberately because "it plays well at home." And that, for a politician, is what really matters: What plays well at home?

A well-researched speech, a thoughtful amendment to a bill, an informed intervention in a committee proceeding—all of this is good legislative work, but it counts for precisely nothing back home.

Behaving badly enough to get tossed from the chamber, on the other hand, is guaranteed to get you in the newspaper and maybe on the evening news on television. You have to pick your spots, and you can't do it too often, but people love a fighter.

Good work in the legislature is rarely noticed, but one bad thing can dog you the rest of your days. For ten years, Dave Wilson of Glace Bay was a fine parliamentarian—when it came to question period, there was nobody better—but nobody will remember that after his conviction in the expense scandal. Charlie MacDonald from Inverness once compared a compulsive gambler to a compulsive golfer. After that, he couldn't say a thing, on the record or off, without a chorus of "Fore!" from the opposition. He was never taken seriously again and lost in the 1999 election to a young future premier named Rodney MacDonald. Hyland Fraser, elected from Antigonish in 1998, had a long career in municipal politics. His provincial political career was damaged irreparably by an impaired driving charge while he was an MLA, and he was defeated in the 1999 election by a handful of votes.

Our politicians find the current system too comfortable to change. It doesn't take much effort to sit in the House—not with all the decisions being made elsewhere and no requirement to listen or prepare—and they aren't truly interested in reforms that will make their work in the House tougher. So they talk about making it better, but their proposals for reform only pick around the edges.

Frankly, the only thing that keeps MLAs in the House at all is the rule on quorum. Business can't be transacted unless there are at least fifteen members in the chamber, so the government has to ensure at least that many members are in the House at all times. Without the discipline of quorum, the House would be empty, as it is during the so-called "late debate" when the quorum rule does not apply.

If they could get away with it, most MLAs would happily stay in their constituencies and dial in their votes.

CONSTITUENCY WORK

Day in and day out, constituency work is what an MLA actually does, because re-election and job satisfaction are tied to what they do in the constituency, not what they do at Province House.

Today's MLA is essentially a full-time constituency worker who occasionally—and reluctantly—goes to Province House for a sitting of the legislature. The traditional role of the MLA has been turned upside down.

What are they doing in their constituency? There are three broad categories of constituency work: visiting, listening, and casework.

Visiting

Visiting with people is the heart of constituency work. The politician can fill his or her day with events, big and small, formal and informal, whose purpose is see-and-be-seen. How many other people get paid to socialize? You go to a market, the coffee shop, an opening, a school fair, a legion, a lunch. Whatever is going on in the constituency, you're there. Be seen, be pleasant, be helpful. Vicki Conrad, the MLA for Queens, would make a point of strolling down the main street of Liverpool with me whenever I visited, saying hello to whoever passed, dropping in on stores, because everybody would see us and note approvingly that their MLA had the finance minister at her side. Howard Epstein staked out the same spot at the Halifax Farmers' Market on a Saturday morning, chatting with people as the crowd flowed by. I heard of another MLA, from before my time, who would hang out for hours at the local Canadian Tire, pretending to shop but really just patrolling the aisles to meet people.

Visiting is not mentally demanding. You're not talking about problems, and if someone approaches you with a problem, you can easily say, "I'd love to talk, but not right now. Come see me in my office." You're just out there, shaking hands and passing the time with people, connecting. This is work at which pleasant, gregarious people excel, in the same way they excel at door-to-door campaigning. That's why we have so many pleasant, gregarious people in the legislature.

If you're really good, you remember names. In politics, a memory for names is magic, and nobody was better at it than John Buchanan. Decades later, people would tell me John Buchanan stories and smile at the memory. He would see someone, cross the street, pump their hand, and ask by name about their parents, their kids, their spouse, their dog. He knew when they'd last met and what they had talked about.

Say what you like about his financial record: John Buchanan won four majority governments in a row. Since he left, nobody has won even two in a row. He was the best mainstreet politician of our times, and his computer-like memory for names had a lot to do with it.

My own memory for names is so poor that I would sometimes introduce myself twice to the same person at an event. And I would dread the question "You don't remember me, do you?" because I would usually have to admit that no, I didn't. People understand that a politician meets thousands of people over the course of a campaign, never mind a career, and only a few gifted individuals like John Buchanan can remember them all. But introduce yourself to a campaign worker as if you've never met them before and watch the confusion and disappointment cloud their face. I've done it.

I tried to compensate for my poor memory with a database in my constituency office. We started with the voters' list and then added information every time we were contacted, whether by phone, by email, or in person. When I had enough lead time, like when I was canvassing or returning a phone call, I would check the database for prior contact. I surprised people with the apparent depth of my recall, but it was just a good database substituting for a bad memory.

I remembered Denis Burgess's advice from my nomination in 2001: "People like it when you visit them at home." The kitchen table, not the office desk, is where the best constituency work is done. Being a politician and visiting people in their homes gives you privileged access into their lives. I was their elected representative. I wanted to know these people, to know their stories and their struggles, to know where government fit into their lives and how I could help them.

I especially enjoyed meeting people, now in their seventies or eighties, who had grown up in the neighbourhood and told me how things used to be. One elderly woman told me that Fairview's steep streets used to gush with water after a heavy rain, and her father carried her to school through the torrents. Another told me about skating on a pond where my constituency office was now located. I met the last surviving charter member of the Fairview Legion, Murray "Tucker" Fry. I met the in-laws of Nova Scotia-born country star Hank Snow, who moved to Fairview from Queens County and married a local girl, Minnie Aalders.

I heard sad stories, like the mother still grieving for a teenage son killed in a collision thirty years before, and who took me into her living room to show me his picture. Or the family members beside themselves over the time and money the father was spending at video lottery terminals.

I visited people struggling with illness, either physical or mental, usually because they wanted me to know how the health system had helped them, or was failing them. And there are so very many people struggling with money problems.

Of course I particularly remember the most poignant stories, but there were a few lighter moments. One time I was knocking on doors on Ridgevalley Road on Cowie Hill, and an energetic puppy bolted out the door with his teenage owner in anxious pursuit. I joined the chase, since it was me who'd been propping open the door for a chat. We ran and ran—that was one frisky puppy—until finally we cornered him in the corner of a backyard fence a couple of streets over.

Listening

The one thing that an MLA can bring to government and the legislature that no one else can bring is a keen appreciation for what's going on in his or her constituency. How do people feel about the laws and budgets before the House? What do they think should be before the House? What's their experience of provincial public services? The only way to know the answer to those questions is to listen, and I mean really listen, to what constituents are saying.

Listening doesn't mean taking at face value every single thing that anybody says. It's not as simple as adding up the "for" and the "against." (If it were that simple, we could elect computers instead of people.) It means building a picture of public opinion from every conversation, every call, every email. The essence of political judgment is how to translate what you hear in the constituency into legislative action.

And first you have to listen.

I hardly ever got a letter in the regular mail, and relatively few people dropped in to the office. The vast majority of the contact was by phone and email. The volume of email picked up over time—a change in technology, not politics—and the volume picked up even more after we formed the government in 2009 and I became a minister. The more my political reputation grew, the more I'd get calls and emails from people in other constituencies, but for the most part, I was firm in referring them to their own MLA. I had my hands full in Halifax Fairview without taking on problems from elsewhere.

I got calls and emails about everything you can imagine. There were calls about all the issues of the day: gasoline prices, power rates, property assessments, and insurance premiums, plus individual experiences with the health care system, schools, and job applications. Landlords complained about tenants, tenants complained about landlords, and neighbours complained about neighbours. They called about raccoons, bedbugs, and rats ("I just saw a giant rat on Olivet Street!").

The volume and variety of emails was one thing, but it's the tone that, in the long run, is especially wearing. There's something about the speed and cheapness of email, and the fact we're not looking at the person to whom we're writing, that promotes our worst instincts. When the recipient is a politician, anything goes, or so it seems. Too much of an MLA's email is negative, much of it aggressive, some of it outright threatening.

It's easy to ignore the worst of the emails, but there's a mid-range to which it is tempting to reply in kind. Over twelve years, I did it only a few times—I'm only human—and lived to regret it each time. The last was a tart email I sent to a group of teachers who had showed up unannounced at my office one day—my constituency office happens to be the closest MLA office to the Nova Scotia Teachers Union headquarters on Joseph Howe Drive—and then criticized me for not being there. They made no effort to be reasonable or civil, and I replied in kind. That was dumb.

All elected officials are used to verbal abuse. Occasionally, but thankfully still rarely, the abuse becomes physical, such as when a constituent angry over same-sex marriage assaulted the late New Brunswick MP Andy Scott in his constituency office. The student protests in Quebec in 2012 included several incidents of vandalism at constituency offices, including graffiti, window-smashing, and the throwing of explosives. Thirty years ago, David Muise, the MLA for Cape Breton West, was briefly held at gunpoint in the Birch Grove Fire Hall by a constituent distraught over his impending divorce. There is also the relatively new form of public protest—so common in some Spanish-speaking countries that it has its own name, *escrache*—of confronting elected officials at their homes. Protestors angry about the cleanup of the Sydney Tar Ponds camped across from Premier Russell MacLellan's Sydney residence during the summer of 1999. Anti-fracking protestors took their protest to the BC premier's front lawn in the summer of 2013.

Elected officials can be magnets for people with certain forms of mental illness. This phenomenon is familiar to anyone in the public eye, like athletes and actors. There are also people who are so desperate, often with a short fuse, that they will lash out at anyone who is not able to give them exactly what they want. I've had them in my office and it's not fun. Because of these people, MLA offices are becoming less welcoming and more defensive in their location and set-up.

Many of the people calling are very needy, whether financially or emotionally or both, and they have a circuit. If they get a sympathetic ear at the constituency office, they add it to their circuit. They know what they need to do to get attention: cry, threaten suicide, talk without drawing breath. I was fortunate to have a loyal constituency assistant, Cath Joudrey, for almost my whole time in office. Cath brought her own life experience to bear in dealing with our troubled callers. Partly because of her own background and her extensive experience taking calls on a local help line, she had an admirable empathy that far exceeded mine. In the end, many people call an MLA's office because they need someone to talk to, and in Cath they found a good listener.

Other people see MLAS as automatic teller machines—if you press the right buttons, money will come out. This is the MLAS' fault. Politicians don't like saying no, so when a parent or a team or a local group comes looking for money, the MLA will usually make a donation. Then because the MLA has said yes, more people will come looking for money, and the same request will be repeated the next year. These incessant requests for cash donations, and MLAS' desire to say yes, go at least some way to explaining the crazy system of MLA expenses. The requests far exceed what is reasonable for an MLA to pay out of their own pocket, so MLAS had to find the money for donations somewhere.

I started off believing that I would do things differently. I said no to the first donation request I received. I remember the shock in my constituent's voice. She'd had one of my signs on her lawn in the election. The last MLA gave money. Other MLAS gave money. Why wouldn't I? I held the line on that particular one, but eventually I gave in as the donation requests poured in.

There was one time, many years later, that I got a glimpse of just how far some MLAS were prepared to go to find money for constituency causes. I got a call from a constituent who was looking for money for his hockey team, which played out of Fairview's Centennial Arena. I asked him how much he was looking for. He said, "Five thousand dollars." I laughed. My usual donation was around a hundred dollars, maybe a little more if there was a team program and I could expense it as advertising. But five thousand dollars? There was no way. Then he said something that made me sit up: "But Bill Dooks gave five thousand dollars to *his* team. If he can do it, why can't you?" I told him that I had no idea how Bill Dooks (at the time, a minister in the Conservative government and the MLA for Eastern Shore) had produced that kind of money out of his constituency budget, but I'd check.

I did check with Bill. After some back and forth with his executive assistant and a conversation in the backrooms of the legislature, he confessed that he'd allocated the money from his "ministerial discretionary fund." I'd never heard of such a fund. I could only imagine what it was used for. When I was a new MLA, I might have exposed this story as a misuse of public money. But now I had a constituent with a need, and I wanted to say yes. I asked Bill if he would make a similar donation to the Fairview team from his ministerial discretionary fund. Without it ever being said out loud, Bill knew he'd been caught. There was only one way to keep it quiet. He made a donation, though it was, as I recall, a little less than he had given to his own team.

When we got into government and I was on the Treasury Board, I made sure there were no more ministerial discretionary funds.

Casework

The third category of constituency work is casework. That's when the MLA goes to bat for an individual constituent who is having difficulty with the government.

There was a time, not very long ago, when casework was almost unheard of. Politicians have always answered their constituents' calls for assistance, but the systematizing of casework as a core function of the MLA's job appears to have been created by a pair of New Democrat MLAS from Cape Breton, Jeremy Akerman and Paul MacEwan, in the 1970s. They saw the electoral advantage of good casework. The gratitude can build personal support that wins votes and survives all political tides.

Before Akerman and MacEwan changed the game, almost all MLAS did their elected work part-time. They were paid accordingly. They continued on with whatever their regular job or business was. Akerman and MacEwan turned the role of MLA into a full-time job, but it took a while for the pay to catch up. Akerman wrote a book about those times, a slender but still valuable volume called *What Have You Done For Me Lately?*

Nowadays, casework dominates an MLA's life. Every MLA puts aside their previous job or business and devotes themselves full-time to their job as MLA—which is mostly casework. At least an MLA's pay now reflects the full-time nature of the job.

I remember well my very first casework call. It was the day after my election in 2001, and I was still riding high. A woman called me at home. (Throughout my time in politics, my home telephone number was in the phone book.) Her teenage daughter had lost her bus pass, and what was I going to do about it? I thought to myself, "Here we go." I don't know why anyone would call a politician about a lost bus pass, but I knew better than to say that out loud. I explained to her that Metro Transit was run by the municipality and that as her provincial representative there wasn't much I could do about a lost bus pass. If she couldn't get satisfaction from Metro Transit, maybe she could call her city councillor. This was a sensible answer, but she was not happy. She just wanted me to fix it, and I didn't.

The nature of the casework varies around the province. In Halifax Fairview, our casework was dominated by social assistance. In other constituencies, the most common calls might be about roads, or jobs, or workers' compensation. In Cape Breton the MLAS do employment insurance and Canada Pension Plan appeals, even though it's a federal issue. Veteran MLA Paul MacEwan used to say there was nothing better than a CPP appeal to build support.

People are hazy about the responsibilities of the different levels of government, so we'd also get lots of casework calls about municipal and federal issues. I was fairly strict about referring people to their municipal councillor or their Member of Parliament, but not every MLA was. For the MLAS who had once been councillors themselves, it was especially difficult to resist municipal casework. Invariably they would complain about how busy they were, but it was their own fault. They just couldn't say no. Russell Walker, who was the HRM councillor for Fairview throughout my time as MLA, gave me a friendly warning when I was first elected: he wouldn't try to do my job, and I shouldn't try to do his.

Besides the belief that casework is tied to electoral success, there is a more altruistic reason why MLAS do it: there are so many people who need help, and there's really nobody else to help them. Legal aid covers only the poorest and is mostly limited to criminal and family law. The non-profits are well meaning, but their resources are limited, and advocacy isn't usually why they were set up. Because the MLA has no job description, everything fits. So when the casework call comes in, it's pretty well impossible to say no. You say yes, over and over, until one day you realize that casework is all you're doing.

LOSING MY SECRET STRENGTH

At first I threw myself into the casework. My legal background had given me good training in how to figure out what rules applied, what the issue was, what evidence to gather, how to figure out who the decision-maker was, and how best to argue for a favourable decision.

We had some real successes, and it felt good. An early win was to help one constituent finally get a decent workers' compensation settlement for a knee injury. A veteran's license plate was denied on a technicality, and I helped overturn the decision. (Then I drove past the veteran's house for the sheer satisfaction of seeing the plate on his car.) I took on the cause of unfair ambulance fees, and the government gave up trying to collect the bills.

The work wasn't always about the government. I saw, for example, how collection agencies' harassing phone calls could stress people to the point of breakdown. They came to me as their MLA, but with my legal background I could step in, make sure they knew their legal rights, and act as a go-between. That was usually enough for the calls to stop.

When you get a good casework result, you've made someone's life better. Your own life is better too. You can go home and say to your family, "I did something good today." That, in a nutshell, is why MLAS would rather do constituency work than anything else.

Over time, I became more ambivalent about the casework. Often people's problems went well beyond what we could help them with. Some of the cases were unfixable. Some of the expectations were unreasonable. You learn there are two sides, at least, to every story. Sometimes the MLA office became merely part of a circuit of dependence. If the purpose of casework was to build electoral support, it wasn't doing that. If the purpose of casework was to connect people with their government, it wasn't doing that. If the purpose of casework was to help me understand what government looked like on the ground, it was doing that, but only in glimpses.

After I became a Cabinet minister, I had much less time in the constituency office. My constituency time was reduced to a day a week, and less when the legislature was sitting. The nature of the work changed too, as people from all over the province used my constituency office to vent at the government.

I didn't knock on doors after the 2009 election, even though I'd prided myself on canvassing between elections. I did canvass in

Fairview for the 2011 federal election, but my presence on the door-step allowed too many people to air their provincial grievances. I had a foretaste of what I'd be facing in the next provincial election, and it wasn't an attractive prospect. Close contact with the constituency is a politician's secret strength. When I fell out of touch with the people I was representing, my political strength was gone.

Most Canadian politicians report, at the end of their careers, that casework was the most satisfying part of their job. Despite my ambivalence toward the end, that might have been true for me too.

Except for one dreadful mistake.

John, a constituent, asked me to be a reference for a pre-sentence report on an impaired driving charge. I had met John during my first campaign in 2001 and ran into him and his wife many times afterwards. They were good people, and I was happy to help, even though I'd never done anything like this before. I spoke to the probation officer and told her what I knew, or thought I knew, about John's situation, including his wife's strong support in his struggle with alcoholism. I heard no more, assumed everything had gone fine, and forgot about it.

It was only a couple of years later, when I knocked on John's door, that I heard what really happened. I knew immediately something was wrong because his wife, usually very friendly, was cool toward me. Eventually she invited me in, and I walked down the front hall-way to the kitchen. John was sitting at the table. He didn't get up. He talked about what I had done to him, and it took him a couple of minutes to realize I didn't know what he was talking about, so he told me the story. The probation officer had focused on what I had said about John's alcoholism—something about which, when you get right down to it, I knew nothing—instead of focusing on the real point of my comments, which was the support he would get from his wife if he were granted probation. My words had been used to justify a jail sentence, instead of the expected probation. The probation officer had rubbed it in, telling them that even their MLA didn't support them. John and his wife thought I had betrayed them. That's why they hadn't told me.

There are a lot of ups and downs in politics, but nothing compared to the sick, cold feeling I felt as I stood in John's kitchen.

It doesn't matter how many people I helped. I can't shake the sense of responsibility I feel for John going to jail. An MLA doing casework is catching only snippets of people's lives, usually when they're in crisis, but I had presumed to know more. When I finally heard what happened to John, he was already out of jail, so I couldn't fight it. It was done, and it could not be undone.

No casework success would ever make up for that one awful mistake.

4

EIGHT YEARS IN OPPOSITION

The story of the years between my first election in 2001 and winning government in 2009 is the story of Darrell's slow, patient build of NDP support. He was good at it, and it showed in the steadily improving election results and increasing poll numbers. The NDP went from eleven seats in 1999, to fifteen in 2003, to twenty in 2006.

Unfortunately, I am not patient by nature. I found the pace excruciatingly slow. I was in politics to participate in government decision-making, not to write letters to the editor as a member of the opposition. But in our system of government, the opposition is entirely shut out of decision-making.

So during those eight long years I had to content myself with constituency work and find ways to keep myself—and my party—on top of the issues and in the news. I found my political home on the public accounts committee of the legislature.

This same period also saw a big blow-up between me and Darrell over MLA expenses—a blow-up that would colour the rest of our working relationship.

BUILDING DARRELL'S IMAGE

When Darrell became leader of the NDP in 2001, he was a virtual unknown. By the fall of 2006, he moved ahead of Premier Rodney MacDonald in the polls as the most popular choice for premier, and he stayed there right through the 2009 election. The growth in Darrell's popularity was not sudden, and it was not an accident.

New Democrats had been terrifically disappointed by the results of the 1999 provincial election. Expectations were high after the break-through in 1998, when the NDP went from four seats to nineteen. But in 1999 the voters didn't let the young, aggressive Robert Chisholm take the next step into the premier's office, preferring instead the reassuring, grandfatherly John Hamm. NDP strategists like Darrell Dexter and Dan O'Connor took careful note.

So when Darrell became interim leader in 2001 and then leader in 2002, he was determined to change the image of the NDP. If John Hamm was everybody's grandfather, Darrell would be everybody's uncle. If Alexa McDonough had been shocked and appalled, Darrell would be calm and measured. If Robert Chisholm had done every-thing he could to bring down the MacLellan government, Darrell would demonstrate his willingness to make the legislature work for the benefit of the people.

Perhaps because of his family background—his father was a sheet metal worker, and Darrell grew up between rural Queens County and north-end Halifax—Darrell has a keen sense of what matters to working families. His political focus was never on ideological battles but on pocketbook issues like auto insurance premiums, health cov-erage for seniors in nursing homes, and the cost of home heating.

Auto insurance premiums in Nova Scotia went skywards starting in 2002. I remember clearly the first call I got in my constituency office. It was from a retired firefighter living on School Avenue in Fairview. He had just opened his annual renewal from Allstate, and the premium had *tripled* from the previous year. Many more calls came in over the ensuing weeks and months, and the same thing was happening in other MLA offices. It was clear there was a widespread crisis of affordability. Having a car, or access to a car, is a practical necessity for most Nova Scotians outside the urban core of Halifax. So this was an issue with tremendous resonance.

Auto insurance was a subject on which Darrell was very comfortable. As a lawyer, he had represented people seeking compensation for injuries suffered in motor vehicle collisions. He had even gone as far as taking the insurance adjuster's course, just so he would understand the thought process of the insurers he would be negotiating with. There was nobody in the legislature who knew auto insurance better than Darrell. It was the perfect issue for Darrell to build his profile.

On behalf of the NDP, Darrell staked out a position in favour of public ownership of auto insurance. Public ownership has been enacted by NDP governments in Manitoba, Saskatchewan, and British Columbia. Once public auto insurance is in place, it is never repealed, even by very conservative governments.

My point here is not to argue the merits of public auto insurance, although I do believe it works well. Skyrocketing premiums hit almost every family in the pocketbook, and people everywhere saw a steady, knowledgeable leader proposing what sounded like a plausible solution to the crisis. The proposal for public auto insurance resonated with party members, too, because it was a policy closely identified with the NDP and its hero, Tommy Douglas of Saskatchewan.

The auto insurance crisis was a hot issue in the 2003 provincial election. In the end, the Conservatives won that election, but they were reduced to a minority. With the support of the Liberals, they passed auto insurance reforms that succeeded in slashing premiums while keeping the industry in private hands. With the sharp drop in price, the auto insurance issue evaporated as a political issue. Darrell's reputation, though, was on the rise.

The issue that really cemented his public standing was his campaign to stop charging seniors in nursing homes for the cost of their health care. Nova Scotia has a publicly funded health care system, as we all know, but not everything is paid for. Strangely, residents of nursing homes were charged the full cost of their health care. If they weren't in a nursing home, the public system would cover it. If they were in a nursing home, they had to pay for it themselves.

Unlike auto insurance, this issue did not come up in a crisis. It was a carefully planned campaign. The idea was Darrell's own, based on situations he'd seen as an MLA and as the NDP's health critic. He saw what was happening, he knew it was wrong, and he set about to fix it.

The seniors' health care campaign started in 2002. At first it was swamped by more prominent issues like auto insurance. After the fall of 2003, when auto insurance reform was passed and premiums started dropping, the seniors' health care campaign emerged as the NDP's main policy focus.

The issue was a winner for Darrell on so many levels. Ending the practice of charging seniors in nursing homes for their health care was so obviously the right thing to do. Darrell emerged as a champion for seniors. He showed himself to be a defender of publicly funded health care, which—like his stance on auto insurance—resonated with party members. He showed he was a force for positive change.

At first the Hamm government resisted, but eventually they realized that resistance was futile. They included coverage for seniors' health care in the 2004 budget. They tried to take credit, but that too was futile. Everyone knew the credit belonged to Darrell Dexter.

The third key campaign that Darrell undertook was to take provincial sales tax off home heating. Nova Scotia winters are cold, space heating is a necessity, and the cost of both furnace oil and electricity was climbing steadily. Darrell's message was simple: the necessities of life should not be taxed, and in Canada, home heat is a necessity. This campaign started in 2005, as I recall, and was a key platform commitment in the 2006 election.

The Conservatives again had their backs to the wall, just like on the nursing home issue, so again they matched Darrell's promise. After they won the 2006 election, with a further reduced majority, they implemented an 8 percent household energy rebate, effective January 1, 2007. The campaign was so clearly identified with Darrell that the Conservatives did all the work, and Darrell got all the credit.

The energy rebate was never popular inside the Department of Finance. When I was finance minister, senior staff would suggest to me every year that the energy rebate be dropped. I imagine that the Conservative government received the same advice. In an attempt to control costs, they cut back on the rebate in the 2008 budget. All that did was give Darrell an opening to promise to restore it. When we won the 2009 election, that's exactly what we did, in the first budget I delivered as finance minister.

Of course much more happened during the years in opposition under Darrell's leadership, but these three campaigns—auto insurance, health care for seniors in nursing homes, and home heating—epitomize the work he did to earn, slowly and steadily, Nova Scotians' trust. He wasn't flashy or loud, but he knew what mattered to people and he got things done. He was the uncle, the brother, the friend that everybody wanted to have. By the time of the 2009 provincial election, all I had to do on the doorsteps of Halifax Fairview was mention that I knew Darrell, and faces would light up. People liked him. They really, really liked him.

FINDING MY STAGE: THE PUBLIC ACCOUNTS COMMITTEE

While Darrell was building his own image—something from which all of us benefited—I found my own favourite stage during the opposition years: the legislature's public accounts committee (PAC).

Most committees of the Nova Scotia legislature are a waste of time. The structure of the committees is antiquated. There is no committee, for example, that clearly covers health, or justice, or transportation. Unlike most other legislatures, legislation isn't automatically referred to committees, so the committee members never develop real subject matter expertise. The committees meet monthly, if they meet at all. They might listen to a civil servant talk about the department's plans, or they might listen to an organization explain how it operates. This is all worthy stuff, though dull, but it could easily be done in more productive ways. For the members, a committee meeting is an easy way to pass a couple of hours. Little or no preparation is required, any real work is done by caucus staff or committee staff, and there is no follow-up. The MLAs collect their per diems and go home. Nothing changes. It is exceptionally rare for a legislative committee to have any impact on government decision-making.

The public accounts committee is different.

The PAC's mandate is to examine what the government's actually doing with the billions approved by the legislature. Effectively, the PAC's mandate covers everything, because every issue has, on some level, a financial or operational element. The PAC also works closely with the auditor general, who attends every session and uses the PAC as his means of communicating with the legislature. As a result, the PAC is usually working with much better, more rigorous information than other committees.

The PAC is the only committee that meets in the legislative chamber, the only committee that is broadcast on television, and the only committee that is routinely covered by reporters. It is also the only committee that meets every week. The golden opportunity offered by the PAC was the chance to direct a sustained line of questioning at key decision-makers. That opportunity was not available anywhere else, and certainly not in the stylized, partisan theatre of question period. In fact ministers were never called as witnesses by the PAC, so the questions and answers at the PAC have a substance that question period entirely lacks.

I was a member of the public accounts committee for almost my whole time in opposition, from September 2001 to our election to government in June 2009. For six of those eight years, we faced a minority government. Committee membership reflects the composition of the House, so during the minority years the opposition controlled the committees. We could outvote the government members and put any item on the agenda, and we did, routinely, choose topics and witnesses that were sure to make the government squirm. For two hours every Wednesday morning, I had a political stage, and I used it to maximum advantage.

As a young lawyer, I had been lucky to work with excellent trial lawyers like Ron Pugsley, Joel Pink, and Jonathan Stobie. One lesson stuck: prepare, prepare, prepare. If you're going to question a witness, you have to know the material at least as well as they do, if not better. You also have to know all the ways witnesses try to wriggle out of an answer and all the ways to pin them to the wall. So I worked hard, often late into the night, reading documents, doing my own research, writing my own questions. Preparation for the public accounts committee became my political focus. When we look back at the controversies that dogged the Conservative government, they all ended up, sooner or later, in front of the PAC.

The first big controversy, in the fall of 2001, was the financial collapse of Knowledge House, a Halifax-based e-learning company. The consequences of that collapse are still working their way through Nova Scotia's legal system, more than a dozen years later. The provincial government's relatively small investment in Knowledge House was a tiny corner of the story, but it was enough to justify calling Dan Potter, the company's CEO, before the PAC. It was the first time he had been questioned in public, and it received lots of attention in the media.

When Conservative minister Ernie Fage resigned from Cabinet in early 2006 over a conflict of interest—involving an economic development loan to a company with which he did business—the

PAC was the forum for questioning the department, former premier John Hamm, and Fage himself. Both the government and Fage had been less than forthcoming about the circumstances around his resignation, so there was an inherent drama in Fage's appearance. The reporters couldn't get enough of it. Fage did eventually return to Cabinet, after the 2006 election, but resigned again within a few months after driving away from a motor vehicle collision.

The PAC also delved into the Provincial Nominee Program, in which would-be immigrants invested in a Nova Scotia business in exchange for speeded-up immigration processing. The program had the best of intentions and the worst of results. The "investments" turned out to be mostly a sham, and the controversy dogged the MacDonald government through 2007 and 2008. A huge volume of documents was handed over to the PAC, and I spent weeks over the Christmas holidays reading them all.

One of my favourite political moments came during one of these PAC sessions on the Provincial Nominee Program. The secrecy of Cabinet documents is supposed to be sacred, but I had laid my hands on the Cabinet memorandum underlying the program. The civil servants who were testifying that day were shocked: How had a Cabinet document gotten into the hands of the opposition? The government sure wanted to know the answer, but they never found out, and I swore to my source that I would never tell.

Over the years, the PAC looked into all aspects of the gambling industry, including allegations of conflict of interest at the Atlantic Lottery Corporation; wait times, pharmacare, and doctors' pay in the health system; pensions, liquor, and gasoline prices; the Conservatives' peculiar obsession with all-terrain vehicles and their purchase at taxpayers' expense of ATVs for kids; and much more besides. Sometimes the PAC created the news, sometimes we followed the news. But always we were near the centre of whatever was hot in Nova Scotia politics.

Ministers don't sit on the public accounts committee, so my PAC days were over after the 2009 election, when I was named finance minister. The best compliment I got was from the reporters, who told me that the PAC was never as interesting after I left.

THE BIG BLOW-UP: MLA EXPENSES

The February 2010 auditor general's report on MLA expenses dominated the news for months and was a major factor in the collapse of public support for the Dexter government. But the story of the MLA expense scandal didn't start in 2010. It started many years before. My personal entanglement with the expenses story started shortly after I was first elected in 2001.

An Introduction to the Crazy World of MLA Expenses

How can I possibly describe the crazy expense system that MLAs built for themselves? How can I explain the psychology that allowed MLAs to persuade themselves that this crazy system was acceptable, even necessary?

For starters, one-third of an MLA's remuneration was tax-free. I don't know why, and nobody else seemed to either. Supposedly it was originally meant to cover expenses, but over the years the House of Assembly had created plenty of categories of expenses, and the tax-free status remained long after the justification for it had disappeared.

There was a $45 per diem for sitting in the House; there were expenses for running a constituency office, with a maximum of $2,700 per month with receipts; and there was another category, not requiring receipts, for miscellaneous expenses. There was also a lump-sum "franking" or postage allowance, not requiring receipts. This was rolled together with a travel allowance, designed to compensate MLAs for the cost of travel within their constituency, but for which no mileage log had to be kept. The "franking and travel" allowance was a large, sweet bonus, in the neighbourhood of $10,000, arriving just before Christmas each year.

Each of these categories grew steadily. From 2001 to 2009, the per diem grew from $45 to $84. The receiptable expenses grew from $2,700 to $4,500 per month. An annual "new technology" allowance of $5,000 was added, which allowed MLAs to buy the latest electronic gear. The non-receiptable expenses grew from $500 per month when I was first elected in March 2001, to $600 in September 2001, to $700 in April 2002, and to $1,000 per month in January 2004.

The worst abuse was the $45,000 allowance when an MLA left office. There was already a severance payment provided for by law, but the MLAs didn't want to put a bill through the House to increase it, so they crafted another way to shovel money to departing colleagues. The mechanism they found was the non-receiptable allowance for closing down a constituency office. This amount went from the normal monthly allowance for three months, to $5,000 per month for three months, to $15,000 per month for three months. No receipts, no tax, no publicity.

Let's be frank: Expenses were back-door income. Nobody wanted to push a wage increase through the House. There is never a good time, politically, for an MLA wage increase. So instead there was agreement on all sides to pump up the expenses—which weren't really expenses.

And finally, there was the rule that anything bought for an MLA's constituency office belonged to the MLA personally. Once an MLA left office, anything in the office was his or hers to keep. Needless to say, this curious rule gave MLAs an incentive to buy only the best for their taxpayer-funded offices. Eventually, that sofa or chair or television or computer or coffee maker could wind up in their house. Not everybody took advantage of this loophole, but plenty did.

But there was more to it than money-grubbing. In order to understand what else was going on, we need first to understand how decisions were made about an MLA's salary and expenses.

Who Made the Decisions?

The House of Assembly, as the supreme budget-making body, decides how much to pay its own members. To deal with this conflict of interest, the task of setting MLA salaries was delegated by law to an annual, independent commission. Typically the commission had three members, and none could be an MLA. The commission would hold hearings, gather information, and make recommendations.

Although the commission's recommendations were to be implemented automatically, the legislature could override them, and frequently did. As a result, MLA pay grew only in fits and starts, and for long stretches didn't grow at all.

The whole expense system was separate from pay and was governed by a committee called the Internal Economy Board (IEB). The IEB made the rules and decided how to interpret them. The members were all MLAS. The IEB was chaired by the Speaker, who is effectively the House's CEO. It also included the Deputy Speaker, the three House leaders, the finance minister, and two other members from the government caucus.

Because of this membership, the government always had a majority on the IEB. In a very real sense, all IEB decisions were government decisions. If the government wanted something to happen, it happened. If the government didn't want something to happen, it didn't. But the IEB generally tried to work on consensus, not on party lines.

Or at least I think it did. All meetings of the IEB were held in secret. Minutes were kept, but were closely guarded. When I asked Dan O'Connor—Darrell's chief of staff and the guardian of the NDP's copy of the minutes—if I could see the minutes, I found they were written with deliberate obscurity. It was impossible to know who had initiated a proposal, what arguments were made for or against, and what cost analysis, if any, was done. It was all hidden behind phrases like "After discussion, it was agreed that..." All that we in the NDP caucus knew was what we were told by our House Leader, first John Holm (1998–2003), then Kevin Deveaux (2003–2007), and finally Frank Corbett (2007–2009). We could never be sure that we were getting the true story, or the whole story, about what happened at the IEB.

The whole edifice depended on secrecy. This was the key: the IEB could erect a crazy system of expenses only if no MLA stepped out of line and talked about it publicly. On one occasion Murray Brewster of the Canadian Press was tipped about an IEB-approved increase in the MLA mileage allowance. There had been a spike in gas prices. The government-controlled IEB voted to increase the mileage allowance for MLAs, but the government would not do the same for civil servants and didn't want civil servants to know that MLAs would be getting a higher rate.

When the Canadian Press story appeared on the front page of the *Halifax Chronicle-Herald*, on October 24, 2005, the IEB speedily reversed itself, but grudgingly. The House Leaders' main interest was finding out where Murray got the story. He got it from me, but they never found out. I was fighting against the worst of the expense increases, but I still wasn't brave enough to speak publicly.

Expenses Gone Wild

John Holm was the NDP's House leader during my first term as an MLA. Whenever the subject of MLA remuneration came up in caucus, he made clear that he'd had enough of wage freezes.

Frankly, I agreed with him. In my opinion, an MLA salary should rise by the same amount—not more, not less—as other civil service salaries. You could argue for some other measure, but in the end, the civil service comparison is the fairest. And yet the wage freezes continued. As a result, there was a direct connection between the freeze on MLA salaries and the behind-the-scenes pumping up of expense allowances.

There was another factor too. The NDP wanted to improve and standardize the wages of our constituency assistants (CAs). After the 1998 election, the wages and working conditions of our CAs was all over the map, and some were frankly unfairly low. The allowance for constituency offices was also under the control of the IEB. So our House leader, first John Holm and then Kevin Deveaux, would go to the IEB to argue for higher allowances for constituency offices. They told us, when they reported back to our caucus, that in return they had to agree to proposals for higher MLA expenses. They would always finger Manning MacDonald, the Liberal House leader, as the one who was asking for higher expense allowances. For a while, it seemed that every IEB meeting was devoted to discussions about how to increase expenses.

But I don't know how true all of this is. I am no fan of Manning MacDonald, and I could easily believe that he was behind the steady increases in expense allowances. But maybe his reputation made him a convenient scapegoat. Since the IEB met in secret, and since the minutes were obscurely written, there's no way to know exactly how the horse-trading played out.

What I do know is that expense allowances continued to rise, as did allowances for constituency offices. The end result was decent wages for constituency assistants, and enough money to provide professional service to constituents. Those are good things. But the quid pro quo was a crazy, indefensible system of expense allowances.

Lifting the Lid, Finally

I raised concerns about expenses almost as soon as I was elected in 2001. I looked at the system and knew it was wrong. I objected at caucus meetings and caucus retreats. Occasionally I was supported by other members of the caucus, especially Maureen MacDonald, but usually I was speaking alone. For four years I gave in to the peer pressure not to speak publicly. I collected the allowances like everyone else. When I finally decided to speak out, it was because I'd had my arm twisted one time too many.

In the fall sitting of 2005, the government introduced Bill 252, an amendment to the House of Assembly Act. The purpose of the bill was to eliminate the MLA pay commission for that year and to substitute a 2.9 percent wage increase, which was the same pay increase payable across the civil service. The bill also, finally, eliminated the non-taxable portion of an MLA's salary.

I supported those changes, but I also wanted the MLA pay commission to look more broadly at expenses. Eliminating the commission and legislating an increase meant that expenses would, again, escape public scrutiny. I wanted to see our caucus really, finally, tackle the expense mess. Bill 252 was just another way of kicking the can down the road. But I caved in again, feeling miserable, and I voted for the bill on second reading along with every other MLA.

But only a few days later, we received word that Premier Hamm would propose a resolution to appoint someone to look at the question of MLA compensation. All of the House Leaders had agreed to support it. The resolution was artfully worded, but the key was that the report would be filed after the next election, whenever that might be. Hamm had announced a month before that he would be stepping down as premier and Progressive Conservative leader as soon as a new leader could be chosen.

The effect of the resolution, as I saw it, was that Premier Hamm was sidestepping, once and for all, any responsibility for the crazy growth in expense allowances that had happened on his watch. The basic structure was in place when Hamm came to power in 1999, but it was under his government that the craziness took full flight. Manning MacDonald and the Liberals may or may not have been behind the push to increase allowances, but the structure of the IEB meant that nothing could happen without government support. And the government that allowed it to happen was led by John Hamm.

Now, on November 3, 2005, it was within the power of the House to restore some sense to the whole secret expense mess. It was time to do the right thing. John Hamm no longer had to worry about keeping his caucus in line or keeping the minority government together. That would be his successor's concern. But with Resolution 5183, all sides were kicking the can down the road again, just as they had kicked it only a few days before with Bill 252.

I knew, finally, that I would not cave in. It was time to speak up, and speak publicly. Only a few days before, I had felt miserable when I voted for Bill 252. To have this resolution follow so quickly, and to be expected to vote for it, was too much. I'd had enough of the hypocrisy and the peer pressure. I told my caucus that I would not vote for the resolution.

There is an arcane but crucial bit of House procedure that you have to understand: When a resolution is introduced, there is a mandatory two-day waiting period before it can be voted upon. The only exception is if the waiting period is waived by all MLAS present. In other words, a single no is enough to kill, or at least stall, a resolution. The premier's resolution on expenses was to be introduced on the last day of the House's fall sitting—a common stratagem by MLAS to minimize public attention—so if I insisted on being in the House and refusing consent, the resolution would fail.

When the premier was informed, prior to the House going in, that there was not unanimity within the NDP caucus, he decided to go ahead and present the resolution anyway. I still do not understand why. I believe he was misinformed about the nature of the dissent. He must have thought that one or more New Democrats were dissenting because they wanted *richer* expense allowances. In this scenario, going ahead with the resolution would expose the NDP as less than high-minded idealists.

I knew that my refusal of unanimous consent would attract attention. I sat in the back room, behind the chamber, my heart thumping. I had never voted against my own party before.

Darrell had missed the caucus meeting that day and was late arriving at the House. When he did arrive, I was sitting alone in the back room. He had heard I was unhappy. We had a very brief discussion in which I confirmed that I would not support the resolution, nor would I absent myself from the vote. I have never seen Darrell so angry. He swore. He was carrying a sheaf of papers, and he threw it, not directly at me, but past me. He immediately left Province House and didn't return.

When Premier Hamm rose, he read the resolution and asked for unanimous consent. I looked at the Speaker and said "No." For the first and only time in my legislative career, I voted contrary to the wishes of my leader and my caucus.

Manning MacDonald, the Liberal House leader, immediately jumped up to take a partisan shot. He said he was "extremely disappointed" that a "reform" resolution could not make it through the House. He said he thought there was prior agreement the resolution would pass. And indeed there had been agreement—among the House leaders—and usually that's all it took. Not this time.

Shortly afterwards, I got a note from Jean Laroche, CBC's legislative reporter and a veteran of the press gallery. I still remember the exact words: "Care to come out and explain your vote?" At this point, the reporters believed the Conservative and Liberal spin that I was disappointed not to get more generous allowances. I walked out to the waiting scrum and told my story. I shocked them, I think, because they were expecting to hear an MLA begging for higher allowances. Instead, I was lifting the lid, finally, on MLA expenses.

Premier Hamm later set up the MLA remuneration committee anyway, even without a House resolution as authority. Hamm claimed the resolution had been blocked, but that was false. The only thing that had been blocked was an immediate vote. The government would have been within its rights to call a debate on the resolution two days later, and the motion would have passed by 50–1. But it was the last day of the sitting, and there was no time for a debate, and except from me, no desire for one. The fact the commission was set up anyway demonstrates the resolution was window-dressing. Its purpose was only to secure the support, and the silence, of all parties in the House.

Was this, then, a great victory? Hardly. The MLA remuneration commission, chaired by former MP Barbara McDougall, reported after the 2006 election. The status quo was more or less frozen. Now that everyone knew there was an MLA who would object, there were no new proposals to pump up the allowances. For the rest of the MacDonald government's term (2006–2009), the system stayed pretty much as it had been before the McDougall report. The problem, of course, was that this post-2006 status quo was a status quo of indefensible rules. The auditor general's report in February 2010, which finally blew up the whole sorry mess, covered precisely this period. It did not go further back than 2006.

I got no support from other MLAs. There were a couple of MLAs on our side of the House who said they agreed with me, but they wouldn't say so publicly. A Conservative minister, David Morse from Kings South, approached me in the parking lot of Province House to say that he thought I was right, but he too declined to say so publicly. This kind of thing was more annoying than helpful. I was under pressure from my caucus to keep quiet and not talk to the media any more. I surely could have used even just one more voice of support, especially from someone on the government side. But those MLAs who agreed with me—and there were only a few—were afraid to break the code of silence.

I heard later—many years later—that Darrell took the whole episode very hard. He left the legislature that day and didn't come back, and in fact dropped out of sight for several weeks afterwards. He took my contrary vote as a significant, direct challenge to his leadership. He never fully trusted me again. I would feel the repercussions for years, right into our time in government, which at that point was almost four years in the future.

THE RULES OF THE GAME

Here's what I learned about politics from eight years in opposition.

Being in politics makes you dumber, and the longer you're in politics, the dumber you get. That's because you learn habits of behaviour and speech that serve political purposes but are at odds with the way normal people think and talk. As the habits become engrained, you no longer even notice that you're thinking and acting like a politician. You do it because it works.

These are the Rules of the Game:

- Get yourself re-elected. Like the sex drive among primates, the drive to be re-elected drives everything a politician does.
- Spend as little time as possible at the legislature. There are no voters there, so any time spent there is wasted. Go where the voters are. Go home.
- Perception is reality. Since people vote based on what they believe to be true, it doesn't matter what is actually true. This is at the root of all the dark political arts.
- Keep it simple. Policy debates are for losers. Focus on what is most likely to sink in with a distracted electorate: slogans, scandals, personalities, pictures, image. Find whatever works, then repeat it relentlessly.
- Put yourself in the spotlight. People are more likely to vote for someone they've met or feel they know or at least have heard of. If it's not in the news, it didn't happen.
- Politics is a team sport, part 1: Loyalty. You can't accomplish anything as an individual. No matter what, stick with your team.
- Politics is a team sport, part 2: Always be attacking. There are other teams that want to take away your job at the next election. You have to beat them, and if you can, destroy them.
- Don't leave a paper trail. You don't want to leave any evidence

that runs against your own story. If you're explaining, you're losing.

- Fight hard to take credit, fight harder to avoid blame.
- Deny that these are the Rules of the Game.

Learning the Rules of the Game

To the new politician, the Rules of the Game seem foreign. Some vow to resist. They got into politics "to make a difference." Inevitably, though, the biggest difference is in themselves. They are socialized into the ways of the tribe or they leave.

Sometimes the socialization process happens suddenly. The leader or a caucus veteran sits the new politician down—usually because he or she has caused some sort of trouble—and lays down the law. "This is how things are done around here," the veteran says, "and if you want to stay in this caucus, here's what you'll do." The new politician has been warned, and doesn't like it. The new politician wants to belong. The new politician wants to be liked and valued by the party leadership. The new politician wants to be re-elected. So new politicians do what they're told.

Usually, the socialization process is more gradual. The new politician watches who succeeds and who doesn't and starts mimicking the successful ones. The ones who follow the Rules of the Game get ahead—with the party leadership, with the reporters, with the voters. The new politician discovers through experience that the Rules of the Game are the best way to handle the challenges of political life. The socialization process is so gradual that the politician may not even notice. The Rules of the Game don't announce themselves. They just seep in.

So one way or the other, every successful politician follows the Rules of the Game. The ones who don't follow them eventually leave politics: they become disillusioned and quit, or they are discredited, or they are defeated.

The socialization process is complete when the politician starts teaching the Rules of the Game to those who have just joined the tribe.

5

ELECTION 2009:
THE HONEYMOON BEGINS

ELECTION NIGHT: VICTORY ENJOYED AND DEFEAT FORETOLD

I didn't get into politics to be part of the best opposition Nova Scotia ever had. After eight years of Darrell's slow, patient build, I'd had enough of waiting. I told my wife that if we didn't win the 2009 election, I wouldn't run again.

We did win, and we won decisively.

For me, the night of June 9, 2009, was surprisingly low-key. Our win was so widely expected, and we had been leading the polls for so long, that it seemed anti-climactic when it happened. Gordie Gosse, my NDP colleague from the Whitney Pier neighbourhood of Sydney, told me about visiting a long-time New Democrat in his constituency who cried with happiness at having lived to see an NDP government. For me, who grew up with an NDP government in Manitoba, it was no big deal. It was the logical next step, that's all.

My campaign office in the Bayers Road Centre was quiet, as it always is on an election night. The work was done. We discouraged our volunteers from returning to campaign headquarters, asking them instead to head for the victory party at the Dartmouth Holiday Inn.

A well-run campaign knows the election result before the ballots are counted. That, after all, is the point of all the effort devoted to voter contact and get-out-the-vote. But you still feel the butterflies. Maybe you got it all wrong. Once the polls have closed, though, all you need is a single poll result to know the trend. As soon as our scrutineers started calling in the results, we knew we had won handily in Halifax Fairview. I headed over to the Holiday Inn.

The shape of our provincial victory was encouraging. Voters all along the South Shore, all the way down to the Yarmouth County line, had elected New Democrats. Most of northern Nova Scotia was orange, including Cumberland North, after former Conservative minister Ernie Fage, now running as an Independent, split the Conservative vote. We won all three seats in Pictou County, including John Hamm's former seat in Pictou Centre. We made no inroads on Cape Breton Island, but Gordie Gosse and Frank Corbett easily kept the two seats we had. We had stretched into the Annapolis Valley, for the first time since 1984, and were thoroughly dominant in most of the Halifax Regional Municipality and up the Eastern Shore as far as Guysborough County. We would later add Antigonish in the by-election following the resignation of Conservative deputy premier Angus MacIsaac.

We had lost only one seat, when Joan Massey was defeated by Liberal Andrew Younger in Dartmouth East. Joan's defeat was later held out to our rookie MLAs as a lesson about what happens when an MLA doesn't do enough constituency work. In fairness to Joan, she was facing a well-known city councillor. There were other NDP MLAs who were weak constituency workers but who swept to impressive victories. A rising tide lifted all boats, except for Joan's.

There weren't as many people at the Holiday Inn as I expected, and the room was not large. Eventually we all got up on the stage, Darrell gave his speech, and it was over. I was expecting to get a charge out of the victory party, but I didn't.

We did not know, as we stood on the stage behind Darrell, that the seeds of our destruction were already sown. For all of our time in office, we struggled against the consequences of two things that were already done and unchangeable when we walked onto that stage: Darrell's promise not to raise taxes, and MLA expenses. On the night of our victory, our defeat was already written. We just didn't know it.

THE AFTERMATH OF THE ELECTION

Nova Scotia had its first NDP government. Darrell Dexter was the premier-designate. I was a contender for a Cabinet post. But the immediate aftermath of our election victory was anything but glamorous.

For two days I collected lawn signs in a rented van and brought them back to my house, and then for several days after that I disassembled, cleaned, and stored them. It was hard, dirty work. After four elections, I know exactly how to make the signs immovably secure on the wooden stakes, which is great during a windstorm but not so great when you're trying to take them apart.

And oh, the earwigs. The sign material was corrugated plastic. The corrugation means the signs are really a series of plastic tubes, which earwigs find delightfully comfortable. Since the 2009 campaign ran during all of May and into early June, the earwigs were in their element. For the week after our victory, I was disassembling signs, and shaking out and stomping on thousands of earwigs. So much for the glamour of victory.

Winning an election is, except for the premier-designate, mostly hurry-up-and-wait. There is always a week or two between election day and the swearing-in of the Cabinet. So my main task for that first week—and I presume it was the same for my caucus colleagues—was to clean up from the election and wonder who Darrell would include in his Cabinet.

Before making his choices, Darrell met individually with every member of his new caucus. My turn was about a week after election day. The meeting was held in an odd location: the bar of the Radisson

Hotel, across the street from the office building that housed the NDP caucus office. The MLAs had to sit in the lobby, waiting to be summoned, with hotel guests coming and going. I think it was Becky Kent before me. When she was ushered out and I was ushered in, it was Darrell and me, alone in an empty hotel bar. It felt surreal.

Darrell offered no clues about his intentions. I remember only one question: What would I do if I disagreed with a Cabinet decision? It was a strange question. The doctrine of Cabinet solidarity says that Cabinet decisions are collective decisions and must be supported by the whole Cabinet. A minister who is unwilling to support publicly a Cabinet decision must resign. The answer was not a matter of judgment—it would be the same for every minister—and so I wondered why Darrell was asking the question at all. Was it just for me? Was he subtly reminding me of our big blow-up over MLA expenses, when I had defied his authority? Was he warning me?

I believed that, on experience and ability, I had a reasonably good chance of being named to the Cabinet. I had done good work as the opposition finance critic, as a member of the public accounts committee, and in the constituency. I had supported Darrell for the leadership, and had—except that once on expenses—been a loyal team player. But Darrell's question during the interview left me uncertain.

We discussed which portfolios I would like. Finance was my first choice. I told him I didn't want to be the minister of health, because it is the one job in government that I consider to be impossible, or minister of justice, because my wife has a senior position there. I also asked if I could be the minister of Acadian affairs.

Darrell did not make the Cabinet calls until the morning of the swearing-in, on June 19, 2009. The only time I remember being as nervous over a phone call was in December 1983, when I paced a Regina hotel room for hours, waiting to hear if I'd been selected as a Rhodes Scholar. I kept looking at my watch, and asking myself, *What's taking so long?*

The call came mid-morning. Darrell had a lot of calls to make and his tone was brisk. I was to be minister of finance and minister of Acadian affairs, with a long list of related responsibilities including alcohol and gambling. Although I didn't know it, ahead of me was a lot of hard work, political heartache, and in the end, my resignation from Cabinet and the end of my political career.

But that was later.

BECOMING A CABINET MINISTER

The Cabinet swearing-in ceremony was a beautiful, memorable event. It was much more memorable for me than election night. The ceremony was held at the Cunard Centre, a major event space created on Halifax's waterfront, adjacent to the national immigration museum at Pier 21. The crowd was large. Everyone who had contributed to electing the NDP government was there, and they brought their friends and family.

The mood was festive. There was the promise of positive change, a new beginning, an end to the old ways. It was summer and the sun was still shining brightly as the crowd converged for a 6:00 P.M. start. Because the Cabinet calls had been made only that morning, I walked toward the Cunard Centre without knowing who else was in Cabinet.

When I got there, I joined the queue like everyone else. One of the organizers spotted me in the line and beckoned to me to enter by a different door. I was shown up some back stairs to a small open area overlooking the Cunard Centre floor. I was the first minister to arrive, so I watched my new Cabinet colleagues arrive, one by one.

I was a little afraid I wouldn't recognize some of them. I didn't know quite a few of the new caucus members, like Denise Peterson-Rafuse, Ramona Jennex, and Ross Landry. If I'd met them before, it was only briefly.

I asked Bob Fowler, the clerk of the executive council, if the oath was available in French, for when I was sworn in as minister of Acadian affairs. They didn't have it—it probably hadn't occurred to them that an anglophone would want to swear the oath in French—and Bob had to call back to the office to get it. By the time the ceremony started all was in place. And when I started to speak the words in French, a cheer went up from the audience.

There were only twelve of us, including Darrell. Our Cabinet was the usual mix of ability, seniority, gender, ethnicity, and geography. The Valley seat went to Ramona Jennex over Jim Morton. The northern seat went to Ross Landry, to the chagrin of Clarrie MacKinnon, who had recruited Ross as a candidate. The South Shore seats, which had five contenders, went to Sterling Belliveau and Denise Peterson-Rafuse over Pam Birdsall, Gary Ramey, and Vicki Conrad. There was a lot of talent on the backbench. It's too bad that Pam, Clarrie, Jim, and Lenore Zann, for example, never had the chance to show what they could do with a portfolio.

One jarring note was the absence from Cabinet of Howard Epstein. He was the only one of the "class of '98" who was missing. A number of people have asked me why he was left out. I don't know. I have never spoken with Darrell about his relationship with Howard, nor with Howard about Darrell.

You could argue that there were only so many Cabinet spots for MLAS from the Halifax core. It was a small Cabinet. Howard's constituency was next door to mine, Maureen MacDonald's, and Bill Estabrooks's. But there had to be more to it than that. Howard was too smart and too experienced to be left on the sidelines merely because of geography.

Howard had been difficult at times. During the 2001 by-elections, when I was running in Halifax Fairview and Helen MacDonald was running in Cape Breton North, the Canadian Press ran a story in which Howard questioned the appropriateness of saying the Lord's Prayer in the legislature of a multi-ethnic and multi-faith province.

Of course he was right, but his leader was trying to win a seat in a largely Catholic constituency. The timing was awful. The article created a stir. Even I, running in a Halifax suburban riding, heard about it on the doorstep. Howard just shrugged and wondered why people were upset, since he was right. The interview had been done before the campaign. It wasn't his fault, he said, that Canadian Press had held it until the campaign started.

There was more. After Helen MacDonald resigned, Darrell became interim leader. On the same day that he announced he was a candidate for the permanent leadership, someone leaked to a reporter the fact that Darrell had been convicted, when he was nineteen, of impaired driving. This news had frightening resonance in a party that had suffered through a similar revelation about former leader Robert Chisholm on the eve of the 1999 election. There was a strong suspicion among Darrell's people that Howard was the leaker, or knew who was, but there was never any proof. In politics, lack of proof doesn't always matter.

Howard did not support Darrell for the leadership in 2002, but that cannot, in itself, be the reason for their failure to connect. John MacDonell also competed for the leadership, and Maureen and Kevin supported John. All three of them learned to work with Darrell. Howard was different. If there was ever discontent within the party, Howard could usually be found in the vicinity. On election night in 2013 he jumped in front of the cameras within minutes of the polls closing, grimly predicting a "thumping" for the NDP. Who needed an opposition when there was Howard?

Of course Howard was dead right about the outcome of the 2013 election. What is not known outside the caucus is that, before every election, he would circulate a lengthy memo to caucus, detailing our failings and demonstrating how our collapse was a logical inevitability unless we made the changes he recommended. I've kept only one of these memos, from just before the 2006 election, but there was one before every election. Each time our seat count rose. But if you write the we-are-on-the-eve-of-destruction memo enough times, eventually you will be right.

Howard is a born contrarian, but I don't think Darrell was entirely fair with him. Howard never voted in the legislature against the leader's wishes. If he had misgivings, he expressed them in caucus and, occasionally, he absented himself from a vote. He did have a behind-the-scenes role of some importance in the Dexter government—he chaired the legislation committee that vetted all legislative proposals before they were tabled in the House—and he fulfilled it with ability and attention to detail.

With perfect hindsight, Howard should have been included in the Cabinet, if not on that first day, then later. At best, Howard would have brought his sharp intellect to bear on the issues besetting the government, perhaps helping us to avoid some of our worst mistakes. At worst, we would have avoided the sniping from the party faction that looked up to Howard. For some party members, Howard's absence from that first Cabinet planted seeds of doubt about their commitment to the party and their support for the Dexter government. Howard's supporters never forgave or forgot, and they largely stayed home during the 2013 election.

There is only one other Cabinet appointment that I want to mention. Frank Corbett was named deputy premier. Frank was Darrell's closest confidante within the Cabinet. Cape Breton also needed a signal that it had very senior representation at the Cabinet table. Frank is loyal to the core. He is not a "yes-man," but if he ever had anything to say to Darrell it would be quietly, between the two of them, and never in caucus or in Cabinet. Darrell knew that having Frank in any room was as good as being in the room himself.

For a deputy premier, Frank had a curiously limited set of responsibilities. Usually the deputy premier will be carrying one of the big portfolios, like finance. Instead, he was named minister of the Public Service Commission (PSC), minister of Communications Nova Scotia (CNS), and chair of the Treasury Board. But these minor-sounding portfolios, which Darrell and Frank knew would earn Frank very little attention in question period, masked his key role in the Dexter government. As minister for the PSC, he would quarterback negotiations with the public sector unions. As minister for CNS, he would oversee all government communications. And as chair of the Treasury Board, he would oversee all government spending. Frank Corbett, it was clear, was Darrell Dexter's trusted right-hand man.

THE WORRIES OF A NEW FINANCE MINISTER

I was the new finance minister, and I was worried.

We didn't know the true state of the province's finances.

Wait—didn't we know the state of the province's finances before the election? Weren't we paying attention? Were we stupid? How could we have made election promises without knowing if there was money to pay for them?

Our critics threw all these questions at us, and more. The truth is that we didn't know the true state of the finances when we were elected, and it wasn't because we were stupid.

It's easy to forget now that, in the lead-up to the 2009 election, we were in highly unusual times. The world financial system started to melt down in September 2008. Large commercial banks collapsed. Credit seized up. Finance ministers from around the world held crisis meetings to try to figure out what was going on and what to do about it.

In Nova Scotia, the Conservative government had not released a fiscal update since December 19, 2008. As we moved into the spring of 2009, it seemed more and more likely that the government would be defeated over its budget. Sensing this, the government delayed calling the spring sitting of the legislature well past the norm.

With the government refusing to release a financial update, we tried to find other ways to get the information we needed. On March 24th, the legislature's economic development committee heard from

Vicki Harnish, the deputy minister at finance, "to report on economic conditions in the province." The committee had taken the highly unusual step of sending her a subpoena, since she would not appear voluntarily. This could happen only in a minority government where the opposition could outvote the government. Vicki attended with a government lawyer at her side, which was itself highly unusual. I was not a regular member of the committee, but attended as a substitute.

"No one has ever seen anything like the last six months," said the deputy minister. "These are clearly unprecedented economic times." But she went on to underline the relative stability of Nova Scotia's economy. There were warning signs, but the alarm bells were not being rung. Further information would come in the government's spring budget, she said.

The meeting was tense and difficult. I pressed her hard about what she knew about the state of the province's books, and why she would not tell us what she knew. She gave stock non-answers and stuck to them. The committee debated whether to find her in contempt, although in the end we did not. For her part, she told reporters that she was "amazed at the political foolishness" that had gone on in the committee. In the clash of egos and tempers, it was easy to lose sight of the fact that nobody outside the government knew the true state of the province's economy and finances.

When the House did convene on April 30th, about a month later than usual, the government was in disarray. Michael Baker, the finance minister who was one of the stronger voices around the Cabinet table, had passed away in early March. Chris d'Entremont became interim finance minister, but only a few weeks later he was out and Jamie Muir was in. Jamie had served in senior roles for all ten years of the Conservative government. There was no way anybody was going to push him to reveal more than he wanted to reveal.

As late as May 1st, the government would still not commit to bringing in a budget. They took the view that another, obscure finance bill had to pass first. It was only at the very end of the day, a

Friday, that government House leader Cecil Clarke stood to indicate that the budget would be presented on Monday.

So in the end, the budget was delivered on Monday, May 4, 2009, but it was never debated or voted upon. The government called its finance bill, knowing it would be defeated and that it would trigger an election. Within hours of the budget being delivered, Nova Scotia's politicians were on the campaign trail.

An election campaign is no time to be sifting through the finer points of a budget. Besides, there was now no opportunity to question anyone, in any forum. The House of Assembly was dissolved, so there was no question period, no budget debate, no legislative committees.

The truth is that the Conservatives' 2009 budget was unrealistic. The main point of unreality, which we learned only when we had been elected and had access to all the budget material, was that the budget assumed a wage freeze in the public sector. Since wages are by far the largest portion of the budget, that was an enormous assumption. No announcement to that effect had been made at budget time, and needless to say, it wasn't in the Conservative election platform.

So when it came time to put together our own platform, we had no solid information about the true state of the province's finances.

Did it matter? Even though I had been the party's finance critic for seven years, I had no role in the writing of the NDP's 2009 election platform. That may seem odd, but in politics it's normal. Platforms are marketing documents, designed strictly to win votes. They are not serious attempts to come to grips with policy, nor are they financially realistic. Starting with the Red Book of Jean Chretien's Liberals, every platform now ends with a page of costing. These pages are parodies of real financial analysis. They start with a conclusion in mind and then work backwards. The numbers are mostly back of the envelope calculations. I haven't seen a platform costing yet, from any party, that makes much sense—except when the Nova Scotia Green

Party, in the 2013 election, said they didn't have the resources to do a proper costing. At least they were honest.

I also had no part in the provincial campaign. A candidate has one job: get elected. I wanted to devote my time to meeting as many voters in Halifax Fairview as possible. Darrell and I spoke exactly once during the 2009 campaign, by telephone, and it was on the very minor point of whether we were calling on the auditor general to conduct a post-election "audit" or whether "review" was a better word. So if I wasn't involved in the writing of the platform or the conduct of the campaign, that was my choice as much as the central campaign's.

Here's the problem with the platform and with Darrell's campaign promises: There was no way it was going to work. The platform promised no reduction in services and a balanced budget. During the campaign, Darrell promised no tax increases.

Keeping one of those promises would be hard enough. Keeping two would be really difficult. Keeping all three? That would require a rare combination of good books, a good economy, and good luck. And we were, in June 2009, less than a year into a global financial crisis.

An election platform is all very well as a marketing document, but it is no basis on which to run a government. I was the new finance minister, and I was worried. No wonder.

6

INSIDE THE DEXTER GOVERNMENT

THE CABINET

The Cabinet, more formally referred to as the executive council, is the supreme decision-making body of government—in theory. The Cabinet meets once a week, on a Thursday morning, in a windowless room on the ground floor of One Government Place, diagonally opposite the back door of Province House. The multipurpose room, as it is known, has no soul. It could be a hotel meeting room anywhere in North America.

The room is dominated by a large, black table. The table was too large for a twelve-member Cabinet and too wide for a comfortable conversation. The premier sits at the head, and the ministers sit in order of precedence. The deputy premier sits on the premier's left. After that, precedence is determined by years in Cabinet, years in the House, and where there's a tie, by the alphabetical names of constituencies. So to Darrell's left was Frank Corbett, John MacDonell, me, Sterling Belliveau, Denise Peterson-Rafuse, and Ross Landry. To Darrell's right was Maureen MacDonald, Bill Estabrooks, Marilyn More, Percy Paris, and Ramona Jennex.

How do you learn to be a Cabinet minister?

The Cabinet agenda and supporting material is circulated a week in advance—in theory. A surprising amount of the agenda is routine business, such as small land transactions and appointment of commissioners of oaths. The agenda can be very short or very long, and the supporting material can be a few pages or inches thick. I'm a fast reader, but still I struggled to keep up with the Cabinet material. We were all busy with our departments, our constituencies, and our families. Reading the Cabinet material always got pushed to the edges of my calendar—early mornings and late nights.

The provincial government is a sprawling behemoth. On one agenda you might find new workplace safety regulations, a health authority business plan, a federal-provincial agreement on correctional services, and a provincial bond issue. The next week it might be a revision to a funding agreement with a medical specialty, a payroll rebate agreement from Nova Scotia Business Inc., changes to the social assistance regulations, and a beef support program. And the week after is different again.

Do we seriously expect our Cabinet ministers to have meaningful discussions on such a bewildering array of topics?

I've already pointed out that our MLAS are almost comically unsuited for the role that is thrust upon them in the legislature. That is doubly true of the MLAS we put in Cabinet. Every Cabinet is chosen based on a mix of ability, seniority, gender, ethnicity, and geography, and ours was no exception. One day you're a regular citizen, with maybe a few years of experience in the legislature, or maybe none. The next day you're a Cabinet minister, and suddenly you're supposed to read, digest, and debate all manner of complex issues, week after week, when each of the topics would be a challenge for any expert in the field.

The Dexter Cabinet started with only twelve members. The point, I think, was to demonstrate more frugality than the MacDonald Cabinet, which at the end had ballooned to nineteen. John Hamm had done the same thing, starting with an eleven-member Cabinet as a way to contrast himself with the outgoing Liberals. But Cabinet size is the wrong way to send a signal. In exchange for a signal that is quickly forgotten, we had only a dozen people, none of whom had ever served as a minister, in charge of a provincial government with a finger in a thousand pies and a budget of over nine billion dollars.

To make it even harder, or more comical, deputy ministers aren't allowed to see Cabinet documents from other departments, so they can't help their ministers prepare. The finance deputy was the only exception. I suppose it had occurred to someone in the past that the Department of Finance, at least, should be aware of what Cabinet was looking at so they could spot any financial implications. The rest of the ministers come into Cabinet without a briefing on how the proposals might impact their own department, never mind anyone else's. When I went to Economic and Rural Development and Tourism (ERDT), in May 2013, I started showing the Cabinet agenda to my deputy. It was the first time he'd ever seen one.

On top of all this, there are "walk-ins." A walk-in is when the premier or a minister is looking for a decision, but the material hasn't been circulated in advance. Sometimes a matter is so urgent that advance notice isn't possible. Usually, though, it's poor planning by a department or indifference by a minister. The premier would also use walk-ins when he considered a decision to be his prerogative, like the appointment of a deputy minister.

Walk-ins are dangerous because, by definition, nobody has had time to read the material, much less to think about it. We had been warned, quietly, that most of the previous government's controversial files could be traced back to Cabinet walk-ins. I thought walk-ins were a terrible way to do business and pressed hard to eliminate them except in cases of true urgency. We never eliminated them completely. In a bit of poetic justice, one of my last Cabinet items was a walk-in. My colleagues, who had for years listened to my lectures against walk-ins, noted the irony.

Beyond the formal business, a Cabinet meeting can be whatever the premier wants it to be. I have read about other governments in which Cabinet meetings would go on for hours, maybe all day. Darrell did not use his Cabinet this way. There were no free-wheeling policy debates and no lengthy political discussions. Everyone had somewhere else they needed to be. The only concession was that the first half hour was kept open for whatever anyone wanted to bring up. Apart from that, we did the formal business on the agenda, did the post-Cabinet media scrums, and then we left, back to our departments and our constituencies.

THE PREMIER'S OFFICE

The Power of the Premier

The concept of "premier" or "first minister" is hardly acknowledged in the Canadian constitution or the laws of Nova Scotia. Virtually all formal legal authority for the executive governance of the province rests with the Cabinet or a minister.

Yet it is the premier, not the Cabinet, who wields the real power in our modern system of government. The premier is far more than "first among equals," which is what I was taught thirty years ago in my undergraduate course on Canadian government. The premier may not be a monarch or a president, but we're not far off.

Why is our premier so powerful? He's powerful because we let him be powerful. And we let him be powerful because of politics.

The premier is powerful mostly because modern elections are focused on the person and personality of the party leader. Since the premier is, by definition, the leader of the party that won the most seats, the premier comes out of the election with a great deal of political authority—and political authority leads to deference. That certainly happened with Darrell, though it seems to happen with any

My first election as a candidate was the 2001 by-election campaign in Halifax Fairview. Around me at campaign headquarters on election night are (l to r) MLAS John Holm, Kevin Deveaux, and Jerry Pye. Amidst the celebration, though, "the bad news was that our leader, Helen MacDonald, came a disappointing third" in Cape Breton North. *Courtesy of the Halifax Herald Ltd.*

One local issue in the 2001 by-election was the future of Halifax West High School, which had been closed for environmental reasons. A few weeks after becoming MLA, I stood in the legislature to give my maiden speech, and "I was startled to realize…that no one in the room, absolutely no one, was listening."

Since our constituencies overlapped, I shared an office with Alexa McDonough, former provincial and federal NDP leader and MP for Halifax. "Because the MLA has no job description, everything fits. So when the casework call comes in, it's pretty well impossible to say no. You say yes, over and over, until one day you realize that casework is all you're doing." *Catherine Joudrey*

Signing the oath as a Cabinet minister at the Cunard Centre, June 19, 2009, with Lieutenant-Governor Mayann Francis (standing, left) and Premier Darrell Dexter (right). "The desire to be in Cabinet exerts an almost otherworldly pull on a politician's mind." *Communications Nova Scotia*

There was a large crowd, estimated at 1,500, at the Cunard Centre for the 2009 Cabinet swearing-in. "Everyone who had contributed to electing the NDP government was there, and they brought their friends and family. The mood was festive." *Communications Nova Scotia*

The 2009 Dexter Cabinet: (back row, l to r) Graham Steele, Marilyn More, Sterling Belliveau, Percy Paris, Denise Peterson-Rafuse, Ramona Jennex, and Ross Landry; and (front row, l to r) John MacDonell, Frank Corbett, Darrell Dexter, Maureen MacDonald, and Bill Estabrooks. *Communications Nova Scotia*

Darrell and I getting ready to respond to one of the expert advisory reports that we commissioned during our first few months in office. "[W]ith the best of intentions—working on core priorities, commissioning expert reports, delivering a budget, figuring out what was really going on—we squandered our first eight months in office." *Courtesy of the Halifax Herald Ltd.*

Leading a Back to Balance public consultation in Liverpool on February 19, 2010. "Back to Balance was…the largest public consultation on finances in the province's history." *Communications Nova Scotia*

Auditor General Jacques Lapointe (pictured here at a different event) delivered his report on MLA expenses on February 3, 2010. "This was the pivotal moment at which the Dexter government's downward slide began." *Courtesy of the Halifax Herald Ltd.*

Frank Corbett, deputy premier and government house leader, and I confer during the first open meeting of the legislature's Internal Economy Board. "Our government's response [to the MLA expense scandal], on a strictly policy level, was as good as could be hoped for.... But it didn't matter. The damage was done. We got no credit for the repairs." *Courtesy of the Halifax Herald Ltd.*

Delivering the 2010 budget on April 6, 2010. Our decision to raise the Harmonized Sales Tax from 13% to 15% ran contrary to Darrell's televised promise not to raise taxes. "The HST issue always troubled Darrell. He is an honourable person, and it troubled him that he had made a promise, even in the heat of an election campaign, that he did not keep." *Communications Nova Scotia*

Federal NDP leader Jack Layton (left) joins me and Darrell Dexter (right). Layton was a positive and popular force, and conferred often with Darrell. Layton died on the same day the owners of the Point Tupper pulp mill announced the mill would close. That may have been Darrell's worst day in office.

Delivering the 2012 budget on April 3, 2012. Less than a month later, I told Darrell I was going to resign as his finance minister. "[W]e walked downstairs to a small meeting room...I told him that my mind was absolutely made up. There was no chance of my staying on." *Communications Nova Scotia*

Being sworn into Cabinet for the second time on May 10, 2013, in the premier's meeting room at One Government Place. (l to r) Chief Justice Michael MacDonald, Premier Darrell Dexter, me, and Maureen MacDonald. "The contrast with my first Cabinet swearing-in could not have been more stark." *David Darrow*

In a crowded room at the Rodd Grand Hotel in Yarmouth, on August 13, 2013, I announced that a new operator for a Yarmouth–Portland ferry had been selected, and that negotiations would begin immediately. "Cutting the subsidy for the Yarmouth ferry was the worst decision the Dexter government made…The savings were modest…The political damage was astronomical." *Communications Nova Scotia*

The goodbye card I sent to my constituents in the early spring of 2013. For a laugh, I included a photo of how I looked in 2001, as a contrast to 2013. Towards the end, "I was swimming in a sea of negativity, and it was wearing me down."

leader who wins a majority: John Savage in 1993, John Hamm in 1999, Stephen McNeil in 2013.

The NDP's biggest asset in the 2009 election was Darrell Dexter. His name carried us all to victory. He knew it, and we knew it. The downside was that we couldn't adjust when his popularity starting falling. By the 2013 election campaign, people on the doorstep in Halifax Fairview would spit at the sound of his name.

The premier is powerful also because he decides who is in Cabinet. He has the sole power of appointment, assignment, and dismissal. The premier doesn't even need to say anything. The desire to be in Cabinet exerts an almost otherworldly pull on a politician's mind. A Cabinet post carries more pay and higher prestige. It's where the action is—or so everybody thinks. Every backbencher knows that any misbehaviour, real or imagined, can scotch his or her chance at a Cabinet post.

As it turned out, Darrell never dropped anyone from Cabinet, probably because he feared that it would harm the re-election prospects of whoever was moved out. This was a mistake. Not only did it block the ambitions of the backbenchers—who are motivated by the hope, however slender, of one day being in Cabinet—but it protected ministers by shielding them from any consequences for under-performance. There were a few changes over the years—the Cabinet expanded when Dave Wilson and Charlie Parker were added in 2011, then Maurice Smith and Leonard Preyra replaced me and Bill Estabrooks when Bill and I resigned in 2012, then I replaced Percy Paris when Percy resigned in 2013—but the Cabinet that went down to defeat in 2013 was mostly the same people who were appointed in 2009.

The premier is also powerful because he is the only person in the government who also holds an elected, province-wide party office. He is the leader of the government because he is the leader of the party. As leader he controls the party apparatus: the polling, the organization, the fundraising. Running a modern political party, with its perpetual campaigns and reliance on big-data technology and marketing, requires large amounts of money. Whoever controls the money controls the election apparatus, and whoever controls the election apparatus controls the politicians. And it's the leader, usually, who controls the money.

The last piece of the premier's political control—and in fact of any party leader, not just the premier—is his power under the Elections Act to decide who carries the party banner in the next election. I am aware of at least one case in which Darrell told a would-be candidate that he would refuse to sign the election papers, even if the would-be candidate won the constituency nomination vote. Whether it's used or not, this power is the equivalent of political capital punishment. Since the drive to re-election is an MLA's primary motivation, the threat of being denied the party's nomination is enough to keep them in line. It doesn't have to be said out loud. It's just there.

Darrell as Premier

How do you learn to be a premier?

I heard Darrell say that being premier is a lonely job.

For Darrell, there was no previous NDP premier to turn to. Former premiers from other parties are willing to chat, but only on strictly limited topics and certainly not on anything partisan. There are current and former NDP premiers from other provinces—former Saskatchewan premier Allan Blakeney, for example, was a particular help because he was a Nova Scotia native and was frequently at his summer place on the South Shore—but care must be taken with advice coming from a different time and place.

It was not Darrell's style to have much interaction with his ministers. People might assume that a premier and his finance minister would talk regularly, but we didn't. Over all my time in Cabinet, I had maybe six one-on-one meetings with him, almost all at my request. I rarely saw Darrell outside of Cabinet and caucus meetings.

I suppose, in a way, I could take that as a compliment. Darrell left me alone. He told me once that there were only two ministers who didn't need regular care and feeding, and I was one of them. He and I openly disagreed only rarely—like when I proposed a gambling strategy that was relatively tough on video lottery terminals, and his response was first to reject it and later to take the portfolio away from me. We were mostly on the same page, but surely we could have stood to have more interaction.

I will say this: Darrell was always thoroughly prepared for Cabinet meetings. He always had a firm grasp of all the material, every week. I admired this capacity of Darrell's. I wondered where he found the time.

I also worried that he mistook his ability to grasp the details of many issues for a requirement that he get personally involved in anything that caught his attention. I learned not to discuss anything within his earshot, because inevitably he would want to know what was being talked about, and then he would say what he thought should be done, even though there had been time to give him only a snippet of the background. He dove far into some issues, like the Nova Scotia Home for Colored Children, that consumed his attention and energy and in which he became emotionally invested. He should have left those issues to the people around him.

The People Around Darrell

There were four men who played key roles in the Premier's Office. All roads in government led to one or another of them. One or more of them attended every Cabinet meeting and every Cabinet committee meeting. If they weren't there, the meeting usually didn't start until they were. They sat at a table off to the side, not at the Cabinet table itself, but they participated fully in discussions and we often turned to them for comment or advice.

Dan O'Connor, chief of staff. Dan had by far the most political experience of any of us. He had played a high-level role in the government of Howard Pawley in Manitoba. Later he was a key adviser to Alexa McDonough, then Robert Chisholm, then Darrell. He is a lovely, decent, eccentric man. He could amaze with his wisdom and baffle with his incoherence. He is not a good manager of people—there was almost a caucus staff revolt after the 1999 election—but as the premier's chief of staff he was in charge of all the people around Darrell. Everything that mattered in government went through Dan. Probably Dan should have been locked in a room and tasked solely with strategizing. That was his forte. After the devastating defeat of 2013, he retired.

Shawn Fuller, director of communications. Shawn grew up in the Avonport area of the Annapolis Valley and started work as a small-town newspaper reporter. This background, along with a big dose of farm charm, carried him a long way: he brought a talent for dogged research, strong writing, and a keen sense of what matters to regular folks. He'd been in the campaign van with Robert Chisholm in the 1998 election when the NDP was a very small operation. Apart from some time at the Nova Scotia Government and General Employees Union (NSGEU), he'd been with the NDP ever since. In addition to leading Darrell's communications, Shawn took on a significant role in labour relations on behalf of the government. He was a key player in the events that led to my resignation as finance minister in 2012. I'm sorry to say that, except for pleasantries, we rarely spoke after I resigned. After the 2013 election debacle, Shawn returned to the NSGEU.

Matt Hebb, principal secretary. When I arrived at the NDP caucus office in July 1998, Matt was a researcher. Like Shawn, he worked his way up and took some time out from the NDP to work for the NSGEU. Matt became the party's polling guru. He was given a lot of the credit in NDP circles for the 2009 election victory, and his advice was sought by the national party under Jack Layton. As principal secretary, Matt was Darrell's top political operative, the one who knits together governing and electoral strategy. To the surprise of many, he left the Premier's Office in early 2013, within months of an expected election, to work for the president of Dalhousie University.

Paul Black, director of community relations. If Paul's title seems vague, that was deliberate. His job was to do whatever needed to be done. Wherever there was a political fire, Paul was sent to fight it. In an organization as large as a provincial government, there are lots of fires, and some of them are infernos. The responsibility would have crushed someone less capable, but not Paul. He is smart and tough. He is also laconic and at times has a short fuse. He and I clashed, maybe because we're too much alike, and there were times we could hardly stand to be in the same room. At other times, like when we were closing the deal with the Irving shipyard in the summer of 2013, there was nobody else I wanted to work with. When Matt Hebb left the Premier's Office in early 2013 for the job at Dalhousie, Paul replaced him as principal secretary.

Executive Assistants

Every minister gets one, or occasionally two, political assistants. These executive assistants (EAs) have no job description, other than to assist the minister any way they can. Their prime directive is to keep the minister out of trouble.

I was fortunate to have very capable EAs. The first, Stephan Richard, was a former Radio-Canada journalist. He is smart, personable, and funny. I often joked that he should have been the politician, since he charmed people effortlessly, something I could never do. Within a year, the Premier's Office saw how good he was, lured him away, and then promptly wasted his talent by burying him in the political bureaucracy. He emerged a couple of years later as an EA to my Cabinet colleague Denise Peterson-Rafuse.

Josh Bates came after Stephan. Raised mostly in Moncton but with parents in Halifax, Josh was looking to come home after five years working for the Federation of Canadian Municipalities in Ottawa. He hadn't been following Nova Scotia politics, but he's sharp and learned fast. His FCM contacts meant he knew more Nova Scotia municipal leaders than I did, and they trusted him. Josh eventually left to work for HRM Mayor Mike Savage, with whom he had worked as a parliamentary intern.

Josh told me once that the biggest surprise, when he returned to Nova Scotia to take the job as my EA, was that Nova Scotia cabinet ministers were working with virtually no political staff. Even with people like Stephan and Josh at my side, it was never enough. It was the two of us against the opposition, against the lobbyists, against the bureaucracy. But when it came to the Premier's Office, I was on my own. The ministers' EAs were hired by the Premier's Office, and the Premier's Office made clear to them that their first loyalty was to the premier, not the minister with whom they spent so much time.

Deputy Ministers

Deputy ministers (DMs) are the administrative heads of the departments. They are the chief conduit between the minister and the department.

The DMs are appointed by Cabinet, but in practice, their selection is the sole prerogative of the premier. Darrell would present a memo to Cabinet, usually as a walk-in, with the names of his nominees. Cabinet would approve it, usually without discussion. I don't know what process Darrell went through to select his nominees. After Vicki Harnish retired as deputy minister of the Department of Finance, I was asked if I knew Margaret MacDonald, the leading candidate to replace Vicki, and whether I could work with her. That was the extent of the consultation. Another time I told Darrell that I had serious concerns about the competence of one of his nominees, but at that point, when it was in front of Cabinet for rubber-stamping, it was too late for him to pull back. He shrugged and carried on.

Darrell decided, at the start of our mandate, not to engage in a wholesale change of deputy ministers. There is always pressure, especially inside the party, to "clean house" and appoint deputies who will be sympathetic to the new government's agenda. Darrell resisted those calls. He didn't want to start by antagonizing the civil service. After all, a government needs to have the support of the civil service to implement its program. We were trying to avoid a mistake made by the Savage government, whose dismissal of deputies started them off badly.

Darrell took a different approach. There were no immediate changes. Over time, though, one by one, there was almost a complete turnover of the deputies. Some of the new appointments were outstanding. Some were disappointments. It's always going to be tough running a sprawling behemoth like the Nova Scotia government. If the Dexter government was going to have any chance at all, one of the starting points had to be a uniform level of excellence at the deputy level. There were always underperformers.

The Premier's Office at Work

I wish I could explain how the Premier's Office worked, but I can't. Its workings are almost as much a mystery to me as they are to the general public. I was the finance minister and I was on all the Cabinet committees, but I never considered myself to be an insider. I supported Darrell, but we were not close. I could catch only glimpses of what was going on inside the Premier's Office.

The real insiders were Dan, Shawn, Matt, and Paul. Darrell also spent a lot of time with the deputy minister to the premier—first Bob Fowler and then David Darrow—and with Rick Williams, the deputy minister of priorities and planning. Within the caucus and Cabinet, the only insiders were Frank Corbett and anyone who played golf with Darrell. I don't play golf.

There has to be a Premier's Office, because only a Premier's Office has an overview of the whole government and only a Premier's Office can take on complex and cross-cutting files like the pulp mill closures and the shipbuilding contract. There has to be a Premier's Office, but unfortunately the Premier's Office under Darrell Dexter gave us the worst of all worlds: a Premier's Office that tried to exercise central control but lacked the resources to do it properly.

The office's Achilles heel was the level of staffing. Through the opposition years, the NDP had often complained about the number of staff in the Premier's Office. Having now been in government, I know it's a superficial thing to criticize, but it would usually get us some media play so we went after it. When we became the government ourselves, we bought into the storyline and tried to demonstrate that our Premier's Office was smaller than the previous government's. The predictable result was that Premier's Office staffers were over-whelmed with work.

To make things worse, the Premier's Office staffers didn't trust the competence or political smarts of all ministers some of the time and some ministers all of the time. Sometimes the staffers were right to be dubious. After all, our system of government requires the premier to build a Cabinet from whatever lumber the voters send to him, and the lumber isn't always of the very highest quality. But sometimes the Premier's Office staff were wrong to distrust a minister, and they got involved when it wasn't needed and made things worse instead of better.

Once the Premier's Office got involved in something, the lobbyists and interest groups wouldn't want to deal with anyone else. Some ministers were left being marginal players in their own portfolios. Sure, they were busy, but often just with the administrivia of run-ning a department, like signing requests for out-of-province travel, authorizing budgeted expenditures, and reviewing correspondence. On any issue that was really important, the Premier's Office would be the decision-maker.

When people are overworked, they take shortcuts. For example, Premier's Office staffers didn't always let ministers know what they were doing. There was only twice during my time in government that I totally blew my stack, and one of them was over Paul involving himself on a sensitive file without telling me. (The other was over the actions of a civil servant who is no longer with the government. For legal reasons, I don't think I can tell that story.) I don't even remember now what it was. I had frequently told Dan that the Premier's Office needed to keep me in the loop when they were working on issues within my portfolio. I wasn't asking for much—just being copied on email would have been enough—but they kept sidestepping me, or forgetting. It happened once too often, and I yelled at Dan over the phone that I was still the finance minister, and if Paul Black wanted to be the finance minister, he could g—d— well run for office and get himself elected first.

It wasn't just Premier's Office staff who would cut me out of the loop. Civil servants did it too. They were absurdly deferential to any contact from the Premier's Office. I don't know whether it's because of gratitude that their existence has been acknowledged, a desire to please, or a fear of punishment. I first tried to explain, and then had to insist, that they needed to stop thinking of the Premier's Office as infallible and monolithic. The Premier's Office was made up of flesh-and-blood individuals, with different levels of knowledge and authority. A call from someone in the Premier's Office should be the beginning of a discussion, not the end, and they should certainly include me in the conversation.

The Premier's Office staff enjoyed the deference they were shown. They would claim to speak in the name of the premier, but they wouldn't always have the premier's blessing. A few times, when my staff was following a questionable directive from someone in the Premier's Office, I would buttonhole Darrell and say, "This is what your staff say you want; is that really what you want?" and as often as not, Darrell would say he had no idea what I was talking about, and no, that's not what he wanted. There was one time that Dan and Paul gave me directly contradictory advice, both purporting to speak for Darrell, and I had to point out to them that they couldn't both be right.

The focus on the Premier's Office, and on the premier himself, means that nothing important gets done without the premier's blessing. But the premier is only one person, and he has only so much time. The Premier's Office jealously guards the gatekeeper function. The result is that even ministers don't get many chances to brief the premier. They have to rely on the premier's staff. Like the children's game of telephone, I could never be sure what Darrell was really being told or what he was really saying back.

One time, near the end when I was at ERDT, I was trying to get Darrell's go-ahead to take legal action against Eastlink. They had the contract for rural broadband in the southern half of the province, and after years of trying they still had hundreds, maybe thousands, of unserved customers. Our MLA constituency offices ended up as, in effect, the complaints department for Eastlink. I, too, as minister, was getting a regular stream of phone calls and emails from unhappy people who wanted Eastlink service but couldn't get it.

I wanted to take a tougher stand with Eastlink so we could prove to those unserved people that we were on their side, and I wanted to do it before the election call. I explored the options with my staff, then got the Department of Justice to draft a toughly-worded letter to start the process. Our caucus members in the Eastlink service area were enthusiastic, but I could not get the green light from Darrell.

In fact I couldn't get any answer at all.

In the end, Dan raised the issue with Darrell at a premiers' conference in Niagara-on-the-Lake toward the end of July. So a complicated policy issue with financial consequences in the millions of dollars and touching on the homes of thousands of Nova Scotians was reduced to what was probably a thirty-second hallway conversation. The answer that came back to me was "No." I don't know what Dan told Darrell, and I don't know what Darrell's reasoning was. I never did get to sit down with Darrell before the election was called. We ended up doing nothing.

TREASURY BOARD

When Frank Corbett was asked in a newspaper interview what he was most proud of in his first few years in government, he replied that it was his work on Treasury Board. I wasn't surprised, but that's because I know what Treasury Board does. But to everyone else, it must have seemed an odd choice as a personal highlight.

After the Premier's Office, the Treasury Board is the single most powerful part of the government. The Treasury Board is a committee of Cabinet with five members. Anything that involves spending—in other words, pretty much everything that matters—had to go through the Treasury Board. And yet Treasury Board is one of government's great mysteries, almost completely unknown outside the upper echelons of government.

Sometimes, for fun, I would ask civil servants if they could name the five Treasury Board ministers. They couldn't. I would ask journalists. They couldn't. Even opposition MLAs who had been in the House a long time were fuzzy about what the Treasury Board did and who was on it.

The Treasury Board members, when we started, were Frank Corbett as chair, me, Bill Estabrooks, Ramona Jennex, and Percy Paris.

Treasury Board consumes a lot of the members' time. It met every Tuesday morning and more often in the months before a budget. The meetings were held in the Cabinet room. (Sometimes I wonder whether the life wasn't sucked right out of us by the amount of time we spent in that room.)

The table was too large, even for the Cabinet, but could not be rearranged to accommodate a smaller meeting like the Treasury Board. It meant that the members, and the presenters, were sitting far apart. The five ministers would sit at one end, and whoever was presenting would sit way down at the other end. I've heard that civil servants referred to Treasury Board as "the dragons' den," after the popular CBC show.

Treasury Board is where many of the most significant decisions are made within government. The Cabinet approves Treasury Board decisions by approving the minutes. Cabinet doesn't have the time, or the desire, to go back over the same ground that the Treasury Board has covered. Once something has Treasury Board approval, it has the approval of five Cabinet ministers, including the deputy premier and the finance minister, and it has the implicit approval of the premier, since his senior staffers attend every Treasury Board meeting and contribute to the discussion. The chances of the Cabinet reversing a Treasury Board decision are zero.

Many of the key decisions that were controversial, and were seized upon by the opposition, were made by the Treasury Board—for example, the decision to cut the provincial subsidy for the Yarmouth ferry, which resulted immediately in Bay Ferries ending the service and selling the ship; the decision to buy and operate a mobile asphalt plant in an attempt to drive down road-building prices; and the decision to reduce the education budget to reflect the steady drop in the number of students. The only time the Treasury Board acted as a rubber stamp was on the big files—the salvaging of what we could from the closure of the pulp mills in Point Tupper and Liverpool, the provincial contribution to the massive shipbuilding contract won by Irving Shipbuilding, and the building of the Maritime Link electricity transmission line from Newfoundland to Cape Breton—because those files were being managed out of the Premier's Office.

The other key job of the Treasury Board was to direct the government's position on public sector collective bargaining. I'll return to this topic later, because that's what I ended up resigning over.

POLICY AND PRIORITIES

In political life, it's very easy to be overwhelmed by the here and now. The provincial government is so large that every day there is a crisis over here and a fire to put out over there. I found this to be particularly true when I was at ERDT: every week some business was on the brink of going under, some negotiation was going badly, somebody was threatening to sue. What the public sees in the news would be plenty to keep a government busy, but that's only a fraction of what's being juggled on any given day. It takes terrific focus to keep an eye on the longer-term issues that have to be tackled if real progress is to be made.

To keep that long-term focus, Darrell appointed a five-member Cabinet committee known as the policy and priorities committee. The importance of the committee was underlined by the fact that Darrell himself chaired it. The other members were Frank Corbett, Maureen MacDonald, Ross Landry, and me. This committee, universally known as "P & P," would be supported by a dedicated secretariat led by deputy minister Dr. Rick Williams.

Rick Williams is a smart guy. His specialty is rural economic development, an area where he made his living as a consultant for almost twenty years after leaving a professorship at Dalhousie. He was well known within NDP circles and was appointed shortly after the Dexter government was sworn in. Rick had privileged access to the premier. He had, in fact, much greater and more regular access than any Cabinet minister.

THE FIRST EIGHT MONTHS: WASTING THE HONEYMOON

After all those years in opposition, and with the seeming inevitability of our forming the government in 2009, you would think that we had a fully formed plan of action once we were sworn in. We didn't.

I had been worried for a while that election preparation was trumping all thought of what we would actually do if we won, but I couldn't find the right moment to express my concerns directly to Darrell. I ended up speaking with him, a week or two before the election call in

2009, on the sidewalk in front of the Centennial Building on Hollis Street. I asked him who was working on the policy plans for the first year of an NDP government. He replied that a transition team was in place. I thought he had misheard me, because I knew the transition team's job was to plan only the first few weeks of government until the Cabinet settles in. I said so, and he looked at me blankly.

That's when I really started to worry.

Darrell had engineered the slow, patient build to government. He was a conservative progressive, he said. He did not believe that Nova Scotians were voting for radical change. We thought we'd learned a lesson from the John Savage Liberals, who came roaring into office in 1993 with a big majority and an activist agenda. They launched into the frenetic "30-60-90" consultation and never really let up. That ambitious Savage government, loaded with talent, ended up with disastrously low levels of public support. In less than one mandate, John Savage was gone, and at the next election, the Liberals lost twenty-one seats.

So the Dexter government did not come to office with an activist agenda. There was no classic "First 100 Days" program, intended to impress voters with quick, noticeable change. Instead, we got busy being busy.

Rick Williams and his Office of Policy & Priorities set to work on the "core priorities" project. This was an agenda of four long-term objectives: better health care, creating good jobs and growing the economy, helping people make ends meet, and ensuring government lived within its means. If it worked, it would define what we were all about when we were asking voters for a second mandate. But this work began when we were sworn in, so of course Rick and his staff needed plenty of time to get going and start producing.

We commissioned two expert reports, one from management consultants Deloitte, which reported in August and again in November, and the other from a panel of eminent policy experts, which reported in November. The expert panel included Donald Savoie as chair—one of the smartest people in Atlantic Canada, if not the country—along with eminent economists Tim O'Neil, Elizabeth Beale, and Lars Osberg.

The House also had to meet to pass a budget. The fiscal year was already half over. So we essentially passed the Conservative budget, adjusted for more realistic assumptions. Even so, preparing the budget and making sure our ministers knew enough about their portfolios to handle a House session grabbed time and energy that could more productively have been spent elsewhere.

And so, with the best of intentions—working on core priorities, commissioning expert reports, delivering a budget, figuring out what was really going on—we squandered our first eight months in office. Every new government gets a honeymoon, which can last up to a year, during which people are hopeful and willing to give the benefit of the doubt. Like a bashful groom, we wasted our honeymoon by thinking and talking rather than doing.

We had not begun to define ourselves before the auditor general's report on MLA expenses came out and defined us, and especially Darrell, in a way from which we never recovered.

7

THE MLA EXPENSE SCANDAL: THE HONEYMOON ENDS

On February 3, 2010, the auditor general released his report on MLA expenses.

This was the pivotal moment at which the Dexter government's downward slide began. The honeymoon dissolved in the daily drip of news about bad behaviour by politicians. The inappropriate spending was spread across all parties. When criminal charges came, much later, they were directed at two Liberals, one Conservative, and one New Democrat. But Darrell himself had made some expense claims that didn't sound right. He compounded the problem with a slow, defensive response.

The auditor general report on MLA expenses was when the destruction of Darrell's public image started—the destruction that ended in our calamitous defeat in 2013 and Darrell losing his own seat.

Every detail in the auditor general's report—every sordid one—had occurred before we were sworn in. The audit covered the period *ending* at the election call in 2009. In a fair world, the previous government would have been blamed for fostering the culture of entitlement that was exposed by the auditor general. For ten years, the

Conservatives had set the rules. It was under the Conservatives that the rules had gone crazy. But in the end, it wasn't the Conservatives who took the hit, or the Liberals. It was Darrell Dexter and the NDP.

THE AUDITOR GENERAL'S REPORT

Back in 2005, I had publicly complained about the craziness of MLA expenses. That was the cause of my big blow-up with Darrell. Unfortunately, my rebellion had a limited impact. The rules were essentially frozen, but there was no attempt to roll them back.

Over the years, both before and after my rebellion in 2005, I had privately encouraged the auditor general to audit MLA expenses. I saw him most weeks at the public accounts committee, and from time to time I would bring it up. By the time the auditor general finally selected MLA expenses as an audit target, there had been expense scandals in Newfoundland and Labrador (2006) and the United Kingdom (2009). It is more likely that those events spurred our auditor general, rather than anything I might have said. But I wonder.

We were in government when the report was ready. As finance minister, I had an automatic spot on the Internal Economy Board, the committee that managed the legislature's finances. The IEB members saw a draft of the report, and we had a couple of group meetings with the auditor general before the report was released.

The MLAS on the Internal Economy Board did not recognize the impact the report would have. We knew some of the specific examples would be embarrassing, but we all thought it would be manageable. In the draft we saw, individual names were not used, so there was no direct link from a particular MLA to any of the examples given. We thought the focus would be on improvement of the expense system, rather than a spotlight being shone on individual MLAS. We could not have been more wrong.

The auditor general's report came out on February 3, 2010. It was a political bombshell. Reporters loved the story, because it kept on giving. There was the back-and-forth with Speaker Charlie Parker about whether questionable expenses would be matched with the names of individual MLAs. There was Richard Hurlburt, the MLA for Yarmouth and former Conservative minister, denying any wrong-doing, followed by his resignation on February 9th. There was the auditor general's press release on February 12th, saying that he had received additional information that he would be investigating. There was Glace Bay MLA Dave Wilson's resignation in early March, which at first was unexplained. In May the auditor general informed the Speaker that he believed four former members and one current member may have committed illegal acts, but he did not name them. The story kept going and going.

Almost immediately, part of the focus was on Darrell's own expenses. There was an expensive camera and two laptops, as well as a briefcase. Why did an MLA need a camera to do his job, never mind an expensive one? Why wasn't one laptop enough? Maybe an MLA needed a briefcase, but why should the cost be picked up by taxpayers?

Later, there was the question of why the provincial government was paying Darrell's law society fees, which amounted to a few thousand dollars per year. It's always a bit of a mystery about what will catch the public's attention, but Darrell's fees definitely did. These fees were remembered by regular folks long after the rest of the scandal's details faded. On the doorsteps in the 2013 election, over three years later, the fees were still top of mind as an example of why people had turned on Darrell.

I have heard Darrell recount the story behind the fees. Michael Baker had his law society fees paid by the province when he was justice minister. Darrell and Michael spent time together as executive members of the eastern regional conference of the Council of State Governments organization, and during one of those trips Michael offered Darrell, as a courtesy to the opposition leader, to pay his bar fees from the justice budget. Darrell accepted and thought little of it. By the time the bar fees became a focus of the expense scandal, Michael Baker had passed away. I don't think I've ever heard Darrell recount this background publicly. To me, it explains everything. But maybe it doesn't matter.

Darrell was out of the province when the auditor general's report was released and did not return for several days. A premier has any number of reasons to be on the road, but I know his absence was a deliberate choice. Like the members of the IEB, he thought the whole thing would blow over within the week. In hindsight, his absence was ill-advised. It meant his personal response to the emerging scandal was slow, and when it came, it did not match the depth of the public's anger.

Our government's response, strictly on a policy level, was as good as could be hoped for. The old expense system was swept away. Every single non-receiptable allowance was eliminated. All furniture and equipment would have to be returned to the province or purchased when the MLA left office. The per diem was dropped to the same level available to civil servants. Expense reports would be posted online for all to see. The Internal Economy Board was abolished and replaced by a new, more accountable House of Assembly management commission—which would meet in public. But it didn't matter. The damage was done. We got no credit for the repairs.

CONCLUSION

The auditor general's report in February 2010, and the ensuing scandal, was a disaster for the Dexter government. The real tragedy, from a political point of view, is that it didn't have to happen. It should have been obvious when I spoke up in 2005, and well before, that the expense system was out of control. It could so easily have been corrected, but leadership was lacking on all sides. The system was cozy and everybody liked it that way.

I respect Darrell, as a person and as a politician. I supported him for the interim leadership in 2001 and at the leadership convention in 2002. I supported him throughout our time together in opposition and in government. But MLA remuneration was Darrell's blind spot. He didn't understand the public reaction. His public image never rebounded. Our government never recovered.

Maybe if I had played along with the petty corruption of MLA expenses, there would have been no audit, no report, and no scandal. Darrell's image might have survived, and the NDP might have been re-elected in 2013. Could that really be the political lesson of the expense scandal: that I should just have kept my mouth shut back in 2005?

The very last act in the expense scandal—the sentencing of former Dartmouth North MLA Trevor Zinck, once our colleague in the NDP caucus—took place on October 9, 2013. It was the day after voters had delivered their crushing verdict on the Dexter government. The expense scandal was a done deal when we walked onto the Holiday Inn stage on election night of 2009, and it hounded us to the very end.

8

SO YOU WANT TO BE FINANCE MINISTER?

The finance minister's office is on the seventh floor of the Provincial Building, the squat stone building directly across the street from the front door of Province House. It used to house almost the entire provincial civil service. Now the Department of Finance, alone, takes up four of the eight stories. The Art Gallery of Nova Scotia is on the lowest two floors, and Communications Nova Scotia is on the third floor. The eighth floor, which used to house the civil service cafeteria, is used for storage, and populated mostly by mice. (There are way more mice over at ERDT, further down Hollis Street, but that's another story.)

When I walked into the finance minister's office for the first time, the short-term challenge was to show the civil servants that we weren't a bunch of crazy lefties. They'd never had an NDP government, and they were worried. We also had to prepare and deliver the budget for a fiscal year that was well under way. The longer-term challenge was to restore some sense to the province's finances.

How do you learn to be finance minister?

I'd been the NDP's finance critic for seven years, but I discovered that I knew maybe 10 percent of what I needed to know to be finance minister. In some ways, being in opposition is the worst possible training for being in government, because you've learned to operate according to the Rules of the Game.

Once you're the finance minister, there's a totally different set of rules you have to learn and obey. To keep them separate from the Rules of the Game, I'll call them the Laws of Finance. The Laws of Finance should trump the Rules of the Game, but—as I learned too late—the Rules of the Game are stronger.

And then I resigned.

THE LAWS OF FINANCE

1. Your government's job is to provide public services.
2. Your job as finance minister is to raise enough money to pay for the public services your government is providing.
3. You pay for public services either with federal money, tax money, or borrowed money.
4. You don't have any control over federal money.
5. If you pay with borrowed money, eventually you have to pay it back. You can pay it back with tax money or more borrowed money.
6. The more you borrow, the more you pay in interest. You pay for interest with tax money. The more you pay in interest, the less money there is for other public services.
7. Taxes and services are the same thing. One doesn't exist without the other. Taxes = services, and services = taxes.
8. If you want to cut taxes, there are two places to find the money: (a) cut spending equal to the amount of the tax cut, or (b) borrow it.
9. If you want to increase public services, there are three places to find the money: (a) increase taxes, (b) cut spending somewhere else and reallocate the savings, or (c) borrow it.
10. $2 + 2 = 4$.

The last one is a law of arithmetic, not finance. But based on my experience, there are plenty of people who think it doesn't apply to running a government, so I've included it as one of the Laws of Finance.

These are laws, not suggestions. You can't ignore them any more than you can ignore the law of gravity. Everything else you deal with as finance minister is a detail, or politics.

BACK TO BALANCE

The most dangerous thing I did as finance minister—and I don't mean politically dangerous—was during the second Back to Balance tour.

I was driving through the western Annapolis Valley with my executive assistant Josh Bates, heading toward Digby. It was the middle of winter and night was coming on. Snow started falling, and it got heavier and thicker until it was a full-on blizzard. We couldn't see the highway. We could barely see ten feet in front of us. Josh was nervous. It was too dangerous to continue and too dangerous to stop—so we kept on. We made it to Digby in time to learn the meeting had been cancelled.

I found the work and travel associated with Back to Balance to be draining, and that night in the blizzard was just plain dangerous. But I pushed on because Back to Balance was the most important thing I ever did in the finance portfolio.

I knew, when I became finance minister during a recession, that there were going to be some tough choices ahead. If we were going to have any hope of winning public support, I had to get out of downtown Halifax and into communities from one end of the province to the other and see if we could find a consensus about how to handle the financial challenges. My job was to start the conversation.

The result was the Back to Balance consultation process.

Back to Balance was public consultation on a grand scale—the largest public consultation on finances in the province's history. My deepest political belief is in the power of the people to make decisions for themselves. Back to Balance was to be the tangible way I demonstrated that belief to the people who had just elected us. I was on the road with the first Back to Balance tour from January to March 2010. I held nineteen wide-open public meetings and at least a dozen other meetings with interested organizations. We received a thousand written submissions, ranging from one-line emails to lengthy briefs, and I read them all.

And yet it almost didn't happen.

It was a battle to get the Department of Finance to agree to the Back to Balance tour. It was way outside their comfort zone. Senior civil servants have become allergic to public consultations. If you want to see a look of horror on a civil servant's face, suggest a "town hall." The image that leaps to mind is an angry crowd, whipped up by the local demagogue who stands at the microphone and harangues the poor civil service souls at the front.

That's why many "consultation" processes that we see these days are online or in writing—anything to eliminate politician-to-crowd meetings. Even where there is a public meeting, it tends to be in a form that breaks the audience down to small units, as small as individuals walking around a series of displays like my old junior high science fair. And even that doesn't always eliminate friction—I saw one city-sponsored meeting on the widening of Bayers Road feature a profanity-laced shouting match, over a map on a table, between a citizen and a municipal staffer.

So I had to push the civil servants, to the point of mutual frustration, to get the consultation process going. After months of preparation, the first public meeting opened at the Royal Canadian Legion in Whitney Pier. We didn't know what to expect. There could have been five people turn up. Instead, there were 135. The mood was positive, the discussion was lively, and everybody left feeling good. Once the civil servants saw the process would work, they breathed out, and their objections melted away.

I was idealistic about the power of public consultation, but I was no wide-eyed innocent. I knew I couldn't wander into province-wide public meetings and hope for the best. There are plenty of ways for people and organizations with self-interested agendas to hijack public meetings. We had lots of choices about location, timing, and format, and it was my responsibility to find the right combination that allowed everyone to be heard and for a true consensus, if there was one, to emerge.

Each session started with a presentation, from me, about the facts of the province's finances. The consultation would be pointless if the output was based on bad facts. And when it comes to provincial finance, few people have good facts. There was one NDP convention, for example, where a resolution was proposed to devote all the revenue from the tobacco tax to smoking cessation programs. Sounds sensible, right? But at the time, smoking cessation programs were about $1 million of the health budget, and the revenue from tobacco tax was over $200 million. When I pointed this out to the resolution's sponsors, their jaws dropped. They had no idea of the numbers involved.

The Back to Balance meetings also included a section where people would talk to others at their table. To me, this was crucial. Community members need to talk to each other, and not just to politicians, about what the choices are. If we couldn't find consensus within a community, I would say, how will we ever find consensus province-wide?

The broad consensus that emerged from Back to Balance was clear. People wanted to see a balanced budget, but not so quickly that the slashing of public services would be necessary. Balance within three to five years seemed right. Any shorter meant that important public services would suffer. Any longer, and the debt would grow too much. Both expenditure control and revenue increases were necessary, but more weight should be put on expenditure control, by a ratio of about three to one. People said they could live with a tax increase, and a two-percentage-point increase in the HST was preferred over an increase in income tax, as long as there was appropriate protection for people with modest incomes. There was one notable exception: at the meeting in Amherst, there was almost unanimous opposition to an HST increase, for fear of worsening cross-border shopping.

Back to Balance was good and real and gave us the guidance we needed. It respected the facts and the Laws of Finance. It formed the basis for the next three budgets I delivered as finance minister. Our critics dismissed the whole thing—months of planning, thousands of kilometres, meetings in communities that had never seen a finance minister before, a thousand submissions in the first year alone—with a wave of the partisan hand. But the Back to Balance process is my proudest accomplishment. It embodied the way I think politics should work: engaged citizens, armed with the facts and in open discussion with their neighbours, make their own decisions about what is best for themselves, their families, and their communities. With the benefit of hindsight, though, there are a few messages whose full significance I didn't grasp.

The first was the complete lack of consensus about which part of government spending should be the focus of restraint. Whenever I raised the question of expenditure control at a Back to Balance session, I would get wildly varied answers. We never solved this problem, and so wandered into areas, like the Yarmouth ferry or P-12 education, where there was no public consensus and therefore not enough public support for what we were trying to do.

The second was that those who supported tax increases wanted someone else to pay. They suggested higher income taxes on the wealthy. Who's "wealthy"? Someone else. They suggested taxes on luxuries. What's a "luxury"? What other people buy. The non-smokers suggested higher tobacco taxes, and the non-drinkers suggested higher alcohol prices.

The third thing about Back to Balance that I misread was the degree to which its success depended on the Dexter government's credibility. When we started, the mood was good, and we were getting the benefit of the doubt. As we saw in the last chapter, the honeymoon started dissolving when the auditor general released his report on MLA expenses—right in the middle of the first Back to Balance tour. After the report came out, I had to address MLA expenses at every session. It was a distraction from the real issues, to say the least.

We repeated a version of Back to Balance for the next two years that I was finance minister, but it was never the same as that first year. For one thing, the Back to Balance program was intended to last the life of our government, so subsequent years were more about checking on progress, rather than inventing something new. For another thing, the honeymoon was very definitely over after the auditor general's report came out, and I don't think the public would ever again have reacted in the same open, positive way they did that first year.

During the Back to Balance process, many people asked me why the government didn't do something similar more often. The answer is that good, true consultation is really hard work. I made the effort and, in the end, I'm not sure how much we have to show for it. Two years later, I was out as finance minister. Three years later, we were trounced at the polls. Maybe there was no value to the Back to Balance consultation process; if there was, it was overpowered by politics.

POLITICS

Politics is About Choices

The government has a thousand ideas, and every day people are bringing them new ideas or new versions of old ideas. The government isn't lacking for ideas. What the government lacks is money. That's why most politics is financial politics. It's about how public money is raised and how public money is spent. Because there are more ideas than dollars, politics is about priorities. Here's one piece of advice from an ex-politician: Never listen to what politicians say their priorities are. Their true priorities are reflected in their budget: what got funded and what didn't? The rest is just talk.

Politics is a back-and-forth process, where the level of services dictates the level and distribution of taxes, and where the level and distribution of taxes dictate the services. Back and forth, back and forth, the debate never ends. It never ends because people sincerely hold different views about where the right balance is, and because the social and economic context never stops changing. The tension between maintaining services and taxes as they are, or rebalancing them according to a different set of priorities, is the basic driver of politics.

The fundamental role of the politician is to negotiate this tension on behalf of citizens and make choices accordingly. It's hard. It's really, really hard.

Politics is About Escape Hatches

Because making choices is hard, politicians do everything they can to avoid it. When confronted with hard choices, they look for escape hatches.

And so do lobbyists, interest groups, and many citizens.

If we're going to get anywhere as a province, if we're going to tackle the big issues identified by the Ivany Commission, we need to name these escape hatches and seal them off. Then, and only then, will we start to have real conversations about the choices in front of us.

Escape Hatch #1: There are Choices, Just Not This One
If anyone is unhappy with a government decision, there is always another politician who is willing to say, "It doesn't have to be this way." And here's the thing: usually they're right. Other choices are *always* possible. That's why it's so hard in politics to make a tough decision and then hold the line.

That's why financial politics in Nova Scotia swing back and forth: taps on with Buchanan, taps off with Savage, taps on with MacLellan, taps off with Hamm, taps on with MacDonald, taps off with Dexter. Each is a reaction to the one before. The pendulum swings with every leadership change, even within the same party. Every government has to make choices, which makes some people unhappy. Unhappy voices are louder and get more attention than happy voices. To quiet the unhappy voices, the opposition—which eventually becomes the next government—promises to make the opposite choice.

What the opposition leaves out is that those other choices will make *other* people unhappy. If they get in, they either break their promise so that the original group remains unhappy, or they keep their promise and produce a different set of unhappy people. Then someone else comes along and says, "It doesn't have to be this way," and the cycle continues.

Escape Hatch #2: Deny There are Choices

The next escape hatch is to assert that there really is no choice.

Margaret Thatcher is known as the Iron Lady, but she had another nickname—"Tina." It stood for "There is no alternative," something she repeated so often that it stuck. That phrase was her favourite escape hatch. It shut down any debate.

It's interesting that the political leaders who are most admired, at least in retrospect, are people associated with resolve: Winston Churchill, Margaret Thatcher, Danny Williams, Pierre Trudeau. But it's a difficult act to pull off and can just as easily lead to being reviled as to being renowned. There are easier escape hatches.

Escape Hatch #3: Don't Talk About the Choices

Another common escape hatch is just to avoid talking about choices at all.

For example—and this is very common—the politician talks about taxes and services as if they're totally independent of each other. In essence, they're breaking the seventh Law of Finance (that taxes and services are two sides of the same coin).

If the politician talks about taxes without reference to what they're used for—a favourite tactic of the political right—they don't have to face the hard question of what public services, exactly, they would cut. Since they've avoided the hard question, they can say whatever they want about taxes.

If the politician talks about services without reference to how they're paid for—a favourite tactic of the political left—they don't have to face the hard question of who, exactly, is supposed to pay. Since they've avoided the hard question, they can say whatever they want about services.

Escape Hatch #4: Invent False Choices

Another favourite escape hatch is to pretend that there are more than three choices for finding money, in violation of the ninth Law of Finance. (If you want to increase services, there are only three places to find the money: (a) increase taxes, (b) cut spending somewhere else and re-allocate the savings, or (c) borrow it.)

Some politicians claim there's a fourth choice, which is to increase revenue by growing the economy, or a fifth, which is to get more federal money. The growing-economy escape hatch is very common, and wrong. A 1 percent increase in Nova Scotia's gross domestic product will bring about $40 million into the provincial treasury. Nobody knows how to increase Nova Scotia's GDP by 1 percent, except through stimulus spending that would cost a lot more than $40 million. If they knew how to do it, it would have been done a long time ago.

The federal government escape hatch is just wishful thinking. Our federal government is intent on shrinking its payouts to provinces, not increasing them.

So there are exactly three choices. There are no other choices.

Escape Hatch #5: Make Stuff Up

If one of the first four escape hatches doesn't work, you can just make stuff up. It doesn't matter if it's true. It just has to sound like it could be true.

It's like being in a locked room with other people. When they're not looking, you paint a door on the wall. Then you say, "Look, I've found a door!" This relieves the pressure, and gets people talking about what they're going to do when they get out.

Here are a few of the most familiar painted doors:

- *Cut tax rates and revenue will go up!* This is a favourite of the political right. For example, they often call for a cut to corporate income tax to spur economic activity, which (they say) will produce higher corporate tax revenue. The problem is it's based on dubious economics and bad history. So when a government actually cuts corporate tax rates, its revenue (surprise!) drops.
- *Spend money now to save money later!* This is a favourite of the political left. The problem is the savings are vague, in the future, and rarely materialize, but the cost has already been incurred. So when a government falls for this line, its spending goes up and (surprise!) never comes down.
- *There's plenty of money if we eliminate all the waste!* This is a comforting thought, but it's wrong. It's not like the waste and inefficiency in a hospital or a school is painted red, and you can just walk in and say, "Take out all the red stuff." Waste is often in the eye of the beholder. Inefficiency is notoriously difficult to spot and root out, and you also run into the Iron Grip of the Status Quo. Even if you do find some waste and inefficiency and squeeze out the savings, chances are it will be a drop in the bucket compared to the spending pressures.

In short, the painted-door strategy works beautifully—as long as nobody actually tries to use the door.

Escape Hatch #6: Change the Channel

In politics, if someone says, "You're fat," the correct answer isn't "No, I'm not," because that only keeps the conversation focused on whether you are, in fact, fat. The correct answer is "You're bald."

There are many techniques for changing the channel, and these are only a few:

- *Tell stories.* The government operates on statistics, the opposition and journalists operate on anecdotes. Anecdotes always win.
- *Attack your opponent's character.* If you don't know how to counter the message, destroy the messenger. Accuse them of flip-flopping or hypocrisy. Call them unpatriotic, soft on crime, partisans, elites, whatever you can think of. Dig up a scandal, or invent one.
- *Put the burden of action on someone else.* One way for a politician to avoid taking responsibility for dealing with an issue is to put the responsibility on someone else. This can take many forms, from blaming victims for their misfortune, all the way down to asking people to put their concerns in writing, when you know they probably won't.
- *Talk about process.* When the politician isn't sure what to do, they raise process issues. They talk about how the decision should be reached—when, by whom, how—rather than what the decision should be.
- *Walk away.* I've noticed, over the years, that when a politician is truly cornered into confronting an issue, they'll just walk away from the conversation. Sometimes they will literally walk away. Usually, though, they will produce or invent some reason why the conversation has to stop.

Sealing Up the Escape Hatches

Politicians look for escape hatches because the Laws of Finance lead to difficult conversations. Politicians don't like difficult conversations. Difficult conversations make people unhappy, and people don't vote for politicians who make them unhappy. If re-election is what motivates you above all—and that is the first and most important of the Rules of the Game—you want to avoid difficult conversations.

Escape hatches are magical answers to real issues. Wave the magic wand, sprinkle the magic dust, and the problem goes away. But like a real magic show, the elephant is still there. It's only an illusion that it disappeared. *The elephant is still there.* Facts are stubborn things.

When I embarked on the Back to Balance consultation, it was with the beautiful idea that my job was to present the facts, seal off the escape hatches, and stand back and listen to the conversation that resulted.

I know now that it didn't work. The escape hatches were closed inside the Back to Balance sessions, but they were open everywhere else. Anyone who hadn't participated in one of the sessions, or didn't like the result, headed straight for an escape hatch.

I don't know what the answers are to the issues that confront us, but I do know that if we are to have any hope of finding workable answers, we have to recognize when our politicians are heading for an escape hatch and tell them to stop. Otherwise we will continue to fall into the Iron Grip of the Status Quo.

Politics is About the Iron Grip of the Status Quo

Our addiction to escape hatches—the avoidance of the real choices in front of us—is a major contributor to the Iron Grip of the Status Quo.

Darrell told Cabinet about a meeting he had with a group of senior deputy ministers. They were complaining about how hard it was to get the Public Service Commission to move on some key issues. Then it dawned on them: They were the most senior political and civil service leaders in the province. If they couldn't move the status quo, who could?

It is a commonplace observation within government that change is very difficult, and sometimes impossible. Everybody acknowledges the Iron Grip of the Status Quo. The more interesting question is *why*? Why is change so hard?

Let me try a metaphor. Think of Nova Scotia as a huge, ocean-going ship with a million passengers and a crew (the civil service) in the tens of thousands. A change of government is only a change of the officers on the bridge. When the new officers come on board, they don't start fresh. It's a huge machine in motion, and it's already in the middle of the ocean. There are plenty of ideas, among the passengers and crew, about where the ship should be going and how it should get there. If you're going to do renovations, you can't just stop and ask the million passengers to get off. Any renovations have to be done around the passengers, and they aren't afraid to voice strong opinions about the pace or the cost or how much discomfort it's causing them. Any course change can take a long time to complete or even to have any effect. Meanwhile, the sea can be rough and the weather conditions can be averse. By the way—you've never been trained to run a ship and there aren't any maps. And every four years, the passengers get to decide if they want you to stay on the bridge or give someone else a try.

Maybe this metaphor is a stretch, but I have always found it helpful in explaining the Iron Grip of the Status Quo. When your party is finally elected, and when you become a minister, you discover that the provincial government is a huge machine in motion and that almost everything is committed in advance—money, wages, programs, buildings, methods. There's not a lot of discretionary decision-making left. It's as much as you can do just to keep the ship afloat while you're dealing with the weather, the crew, and the passengers.

The truth is the provincial budget, in any given year, is virtually identical to the budget of the year before. My guess is that the budget is 98 percent the same from one year to the next. The only reason we might believe otherwise is that politics requires that differences be exaggerated. From one year to the next, no matter who is in government, and even if there is a change of government, the same civil servants do the same work the same way they did it the previous year.

The status quo has an iron grip because every piece of public spending benefits someone. There is no program that is so obviously a waste of money that everyone will agree that it should be cut—a point brought home to me during the Back to Balance consultation.

When the Hamm government was elected in 1999, it launched a comprehensive program review, buying into the idea that there was lots of waste in government and all it had to do was go and look for it. The Hamm government would cut it, get the kudos, and have lots of money for the good stuff. Eleven hundred spending programs were catalogued and precisely three ended up being eliminated. One was to sell the government's airplane. (Apparently nobody was ready to go to bat for the airplane.) The other two were similarly minor—closure of the government bookstore and ending a subsidy for agricultural limestone. The other 1,097 programs stayed in place.

The status quo has an iron grip because everyone who benefits from the status quo knows who they are and will ferociously defend what they have or what they're doing, while those who may benefit from a change do not necessarily know who they are and so are silent. The beneficiaries may be a community, an organization, a group sharing a certain characteristic, or even just the staff who administer the program.

The status quo has an iron grip because routines build up around every process and harden into habits and even into rights. Citizens, contractors, and civil servants get used to a certain service being offered in a certain place at a certain time in a certain way. Comfortable patterns develop, like work schedules or driving routines. Any change imposes a transaction cost. The patterns can go beyond comfort, to things like how much we earn and how predictable our income stream is, to how much things cost, to where we live. Resisting change is about imposing order in our lives and keeping order. Resistance can be acute when it's "the government" that's imposing a change, both because citizens feel they have some control over their government and because there are plenty of examples of change being cancelled if enough resistance is mounted.

Because of the "stickiness" of the status quo, the government faces a battle over every change. A government can withstand only so many of these battles. It's wearing mentally and physically. One time I heard Darrell ask Maureen MacDonald, his health minister, to undertake a certain change, and she responded with a flat no. She was already fighting enough battles, she said, and she couldn't face another one, no matter how sensible the change appeared to be.

Through all the battles, the status quo beckons enticingly, like the Sirens singing to seafarers, saying, "You don't have to go through this. Stop fighting. Go with the flow. Stick with the status quo." And that, in the end, is what most governments do.

9

THE CHOICES WE MADE: BALANCE, SPENDING, TAXES

BALANCING THE BUDGET

The single most important policy choice made by the Dexter government was to balance the budget. That choice—and the hunt for jobs—framed everything else that we did.

Striving for balance was the right choice. Fiscal discipline—whether at home, in a business or non-profit, or in a government—is a good thing. When the finances make sense, anything is possible. When the finances stop making sense, everything starts to fall apart.

There's something that comes undone in politicians' heads when they are put in charge of other people's money. I support balanced budgets because it is the only thing—the *only* thing—that counters the political impulse to spend. As soon as you open the door to a deficit, all discipline is lost. There is no political difference between a small deficit and a moderate deficit and a large deficit. Politically, they're the same.

The connection of spending to votes is a very inexact science. All politicians believe there's some connection, but nobody has yet been able to explain what it is. Since they're not sure how to connect spending and votes, their incentive is to spend as much as possible as visibly as possible. It's exactly what would happen if you had a contest to see who could make the most spaghetti stick to the wall, but without any idea of what makes spaghetti stick—pretty soon the wall, and the floor, and the ceiling, would be covered in spaghetti. If someone else is paying for the spaghetti and someone else is cleaning up, why hold back?

There are other reasons why spending is popular. Of the three fiscal choices—raise taxes, cut spending, run a deficit—the path of least resistance is to run a deficit. It is the political equivalent of "Buy now, pay later" at the furniture store. It's an attractive option because there is nobody to speak for the future citizens who will pay for it. This, more than anything, explains the mountain of debt we have inherited and to which we continue to add. Intergenerational equity—the fairness to our children and grandchildren of the debt we're leaving for them—is the biggest unaddressed issue in our politics.

All politicians have incentives to overspend, but New Democrats, in particular, have to fight a stereotype that they're not good with money. For the longest time, the stereotype was reduced to two short words—"Bob Rae." It seemed to explain everything. Fortunately, the Liberals had to drop their references to the mythical Bob Rae when the real Bob Rae re-entered Parliament as a Liberal and, eventually, became their interim leader. The fact is that the NDP's record of financial management, starting with Tommy Douglas's CCF government in Saskatchewan, is comparable to any other party, and possibly better.

But there was more to the balanced-budget commitment than fighting a stereotype.

During the Back to Balance consultations, the view was virtually unanimous that a balanced budget is important. The only question, given the recession, was how long it should take to achieve it. The consensus was three to five years. A few people said a shorter time, and a few said longer, but in every community, the broad majority said three to five years sounded right.

The drive to a balanced budget was the right thing to do—but it was never intended to be the thing we went to the polls on in 2013.

REDUCING EXPENDITURE

The Choices We Had in Front of Us

Once you've made the commitment to balance the budget, you have to take a look at both your spending and your revenue. The Back to Balance consultation had told us that people expected us to put more weight on the spending side, by a ratio of about three to one over the revenue side.

Some expenditure control is easy. When I walked into the minister's office, the office had its own television with cable service. Cut. The minister got his own newspaper. Cut. Ministers didn't need a ministerial car, when they could drive their own. Cut. That's the penny-ante stuff, but the symbolism matters.

A Treasury Board directive went out to eliminate so-called "March madness," which is when unspent budgets are used up in a flurry of year-end expenditure. March madness had become an engrained habit in the civil service, especially under the previous government. Some years it could be in the tens of millions of dollars, even hundreds of millions, and it rightly drives taxpayers crazy. Cut.

Other expenditure control takes time to find. For example, we were well into our second budget when we started hearing in Treasury Board about "funded vacancies," and I asked what that was. It's a civil service term for positions that get a budget allocation, but that everybody knows will stay empty over the course of the year. It's one way that deputy ministers pad their budgets. Cut.

Sometimes all you can do is restrain spending. We immediately asked for two years of 1 percent wage settlements from the public sector unions. We knew that a wage freeze would buy us a fight, and maybe a strike. The unions grudgingly accepted. They knew there was no public appetite for increases like the 2.9 percent annual pattern established under the previous government. Those days were over, and they knew it. They had also feared a wage freeze, and 2 percent over two years was better than nothing. But these kinds of negotiated settlements tend only to push back wage demands, like a coiled spring. The demand to "catch up" would come later.

Efficiencies are always a good thing—who can argue with the same services at a lower cost or better services at the same cost?—but they are difficult to achieve. Our collaborative emergency centre initiative, for example, was an outstanding success from a policy point of view. The idea behind CECs is simple—set up a multidisciplinary team to provide health care services better and faster than the traditional model of a rural hospital emergency room. The idea was sparked by Dr. John Ross, an ER doctor, and led by health minister Maureen MacDonald. The first CEC opened in Parrsboro in 2011, and more followed. The communities that got them loved them, and other provinces studied and copied them. CECs should have been an easy sell, but I know Maureen found the process draining. The existing emergency-room system hadn't worked in smaller hospitals for years, but the Iron Grip of the Status Quo meant that there was stiff resistance to change, especially from the nurses' union. The move to CECs took far more time and effort than it should have.

Not everything can be carefully planned. Take the paper mills in Point Tupper and Liverpool. When their closures were announced, I don't remember anybody coming to the Cabinet and saying "Should we save the mills?" It was just taken for granted that we would try. An outright closure was too much to take for Liverpool and Point Tupper and a wide area around them. There had to be some sort of upper financial limit, but it wasn't sketched out in advance, and the final bill was large. The mill file was our government at its best—the best people doing the best work of which the provincial government was capable—but I do understand that the final mill bill tested the public's limits for how far a government should go to save jobs.

That left us with program cuts. As I discovered on the Back to Balance tour, there is no consensus, not even remotely, on which government programs should be cut.

I have my own list. Why do we have an Office of Gaelic Affairs, established in 2006 by the MacDonald government and costing $500,000 annually? Why do we subsidize horse-racing to the tune of $1 million every year? If it were up to me, I'd cut this spending tomorrow, and lots more like it. So why didn't the Treasury Board cut them when I was the finance minister? Politics.

The defenders of Gaelic are few but passionate. They'll make life miserable for any politician or party who advocates ending the Gaelic affairs program. Many of Nova Scotia's Gaelic speakers live in Inverness County, but also in Antigonish County, which the NDP had won for the first time in the 2009 by-election. Was it really worth it, for 0.005 percent of the provincial budget, to enrage a few hundred people in a marginal seat? No. We lost Antigonish anyway in the 2013 election and never had a hope in Inverness. There's no way to know how the Gaelic speakers voted.

The defenders of the horse-racing industry are also few but passionate. It's a way of life, they say, a rural industry that city folks like me can't understand. They, too, will make life miserable for any politician or party who says the industry has to stand on its own or shut down. And is it really worth it, for the 0.01 percent of the provincial budget? Again: No. We can look to Ontario to see what would happen. The 2012 Ontario provincial budget drastically cut financial support for their horse-racing industry. The industry mobilized against it, citing all the expected arguments about rural jobs and the rural way of life. The Ontario government eventually backed down, but not without taking considerable political damage.

We could go down my list, or down your list, and have endless debates about what's worthwhile and what isn't. Here's the point: Everyone's list is different. Without consensus, the backlash usually isn't worth the fight. If anybody's unhappy, the opposition will simply promise to reverse the cut. And that's exactly what they did—just as we had done when we were in their shoes.

And then there was the Yarmouth ferry. It was just one decision, but the thought process is a good example of our entire approach to spending control.

The Choice We Made: Cutting the Yarmouth Ferry

Cutting the subsidy for the Yarmouth ferry was the worst decision the Dexter government made—if "worst" is measured by the ratio of financial savings to political damage. The savings were modest, about $6 million annually, or 0.07 percent of a $9.5 billion budget. The political damage was astronomical. A New Democrat will not be elected again in Yarmouth County for a generation at least.

Here's how the decision was made.

The Treasury Board is the Cabinet committee that puts a budget together and decides what will be funded and what won't. Treasury Board staff, in consultation with departmental staff, were asked to develop a list of items that could be considered for cutting.

The first list that we saw included cutting a bunch of small grants to community organizations. The community grants very likely weren't achieving their intended purposes. There was no principled policy objective. These were the accumulation of many years of constituency-level grants to keep this or that organization alive or this or that building open. We started by taking the list seriously, and we spent quite a lot of time on it, but in the end, it dawned on us that the savings would be miniscule and the damage to the organizations—and our colleagues, the local MLAs—would be large. We told the Treasury Board staff to come back with a different kind of list. We were looking for whales, not baby seals or minnows.

I also urged my colleagues and staff to resist the urge to find all the savings by shaving nickels and dimes from every program. The cost pressure in government comes from having so many programs.

They all start with a noble purpose and sometimes with adequate funding. Over time, and through many periods of restraint, they are whittled and whittled until they become a shadow of what they were intended to be. But if anyone talks about actually ending the program, the original noble purpose is trotted out as justification for keeping it. Stakeholders rally. The Iron Grip of the Status Quo kicks in.

It was in this context that the Treasury Board met to consider the new list put forward by the civil service. The subsidy for the Yarmouth ferry was on the list.

We learned that postwar ferry service had been established between Yarmouth and Maine in 1956. At first it was operated by the federal government, and from time to time a privately-owned ferry would run as well. The postwar years were good for the Yarmouth ferry, with the baby boom generation growing up and automobile touring in vogue. The road network in Nova Scotia, New Brunswick, and Maine wasn't as developed as it is today, so alternatives to the ferry weren't as attractive. Southwest Nova Scotia's tourism industry grew up around the ferry traffic.

As highways were built, and as demographics changed, the ferry became a less attractive option. Passenger numbers dropped steadily, and by 1997 the federal government wanted out. Bay Ferries took over the MV *Bluenose*, but without a federal subsidy. In 1998, Bay Ferries added *The Cat*, a high-speed catamaran that cut crossing times.

Passenger levels were eroding steadily anyway, but the events of September 11, 2001, caused a drastic change in American travel patterns. The last private ferry, the MS *Scotia Prince*, cancelled its 2005 season amid controversy in Portland and never returned. The *Bluenose* stopped running too. In 2007, the provincial government agreed to step in to help Bay Ferries with The Cat's operating costs, but the federal government stayed out.

The declining ferry passenger numbers also meant that there had been little investment in the southwest's tourism infrastructure. By

2007, the area's accommodations were mostly tired and unappealing. A ferry schedule change in 2007, which meant that passengers would no longer need to stay overnight in Yarmouth to catch an early-morning crossing, caused further consternation.

By the time we came into government, the ferry service needed the subsidy to survive. The passenger numbers had fallen dramatically since the ferry's heyday, and the trend was not promising.

I was in the room when the decision was made to end the ferry subsidy. I was for it, like everyone else on the Treasury Board and the staff from the Premier's Office. I did say that I thought the area needed a year's grace to get used to the idea. An immediate, unexpected end to the service was too fast. If that idea had been adopted, the public outcry would probably have been enough for us to reverse the decision. But my colleagues thought it best to carry the decision through. I also said that we needed to talk it over with Sterling Belliveau, the Shelburne MLA and our Cabinet colleague, who was best placed to gauge the likely public reaction in Yarmouth County. I sat down with him before our next Cabinet meeting. He wasn't thrilled about the idea, but he understood the rationale. As a long-time lobster fisherman, he knew that it was the Digby ferry that was critical to the commercial fishery.

Once Bay Ferries was notified that the subsidy would be cut, they announced immediately that the ferry service would end. Yarmouth was stunned.

The front-line minister on the ferry decision was Percy Paris at ERDT. Percy was having a tough go in the southwest anyway, what with the unravelling of the regional development authority and his long-standing fraught relationship with Yarmouth MLA Richard Hurlburt. On top of this, Percy was handed the nearly impossible task of communicating a solution that was shocking in its abruptness. He did his best, but eventually the friction became too much for him, and by the time he stepped down as minister in 2013, he had essentially stopped going to Yarmouth County.

Meanwhile, I was on my Back to Balance tour, and it took me to Yarmouth on February 19, 2010. The gym at the Burridge Campus of the NSCC was full, including a contingent of ferry workers with protest signs. By coincidence Richard Hurlburt had resigned as MLA only ten days before, in the wake of the auditor general's expense report. I half-expected the crowd to be angry and unruly, but I still didn't understand the people of Yarmouth. Everyone who spoke was thoughtful and gracious. During the breakout sessions I went and sat with the ferry workers and listened to them. I think they appreciated that. Back in my room at the Rodd Grand that night, I stood for a long time at the window, staring down Main Street and out toward Cape Forchu, glad that I'd made it through the meeting and wondering if we were doing the right thing.

The fundamental problem with our ferry decision was that we were solving a problem that the people of the southwest didn't know they had. Only a handful of people had a full appreciation of the long-term trend in ferry passengers. The *Yarmouth Vanguard* was, in 2007 and 2008, full of articles quoting business owners bitterly complaining about the schedule change in 2007 that had caused a steep drop in the number of people staying overnight in Yarmouth. But the ferry was still running and so the majority of people, it appears, hadn't registered just what the numbers were.

After *The Cat* stopped running, business impacts were claimed throughout the southwest, up the South Shore and the Annapolis Valley, and even up the Eastern Shore and into Cape Breton. Most of these claims couldn't be proven, but we couldn't specifically disprove them either. If an operator in Cape Breton said there were fewer bus tours than there used to be, and it was because of the ferry, that was accepted as a fact. If we said that the number of tourists arriving in Nova Scotia was the same or even slightly higher, or that the number of bus tours was going down everywhere across North America and not just in Nova Scotia, that was dismissed as government spin.

We, the members of the Treasury Board, made the decision to cut the ferry subsidy while sitting in a windowless meeting room in downtown Halifax. What we didn't take into account was that the ferry link to the United States is part of how Yarmouth sees itself and understands itself. The railway was gone. Bus service was gone. Air service was gone. We weren't responsible for any of that. The only link left, and the link by which Yarmouth understood its place in the world, was the ferry. The NDP cut that, and so we were held responsible for it all. The NDP carried the entire freight for an issue that had—in demographics, travel patterns, border security, tourist infrastructure, terminal facilities, and scheduling—been building for many years.

When I returned to Cabinet in May 2013, replacing Percy at ERDT, the only request that Darrell made of me was to pay particular attention to the southwest. He hoped that a new minister might be able to take a fresh look and make a fresh start.

The ferry decision wasn't the only restraint decision we made, but it was one of the most controversial. I've dwelled on it here as an example of the Dexter government's thought process. We tried to do the right thing, and we got it all emotionally and politically wrong.

RAISING MORE REVENUE

The Choices We Had in Front of Us

We knew we weren't going to get all the way to balance solely on the spending side. We knew we had to increase our revenue—and "increase our revenue" is a pleasant way of saying we had to raise taxes.

It's almost impossible to have a sensible conversation about taxes. The right-wingers have so successfully demonized the word "tax" that you have lost, from the beginning, any conversation that includes the word. Thus one of the techniques used by the federal Conservatives in the period 2008–2013 to kill an expansion of the Canada Pension Plan was to refer to CPP as a payroll tax (which it isn't). Similarly, the McNeil Liberals in opposition needed to find a way to reduce power bills, and hit on the idea of referring to the efficiency charge as "the NDP electricity tax" (which it isn't). Stéphane Dion's career as federal Liberal leader ended over his principled but easy-to-caricature advocacy of a carbon tax. How are you supposed to provide public services if you can't have a sensible conversation about how to pay for them?

We looked at our options, and there weren't many. User fees are easy to justify. It seems fair that the people who use a service are the ones who pay for it. The total revenue from fees is relatively low, though, so they will always be a small part of the revenue picture. Tolls are an excellent way to get things built. The Cobequid Pass linking Truro and Amherst is a toll highway. The highway was built quickly, and built well, because of the guaranteed revenue of the toll. The people of Cumberland County, though, didn't forgive the Liberals for a long time. After the toll was imposed, it took almost twenty years for another Liberal to be elected in Cumberland County. The lesson that every Nova Scotia politician learned was simple: If you want to be elected, never talk about tolls.

Besides tolls and fees, what were our choices? Tobacco tax could go up—and many people argued during Back to Balance that it should be doubled or tripled—but there is a serious issue with illegal cigarettes and enforcement. The same goes for alcohol. There is a limit to how far the sin taxes can go up before you've created a playground for criminals. Gasoline tax could go up, but there's no way any politician who wants to get re-elected is going to raise gasoline taxes. We'd been strongly warned, during the Back to Balance consultations, not to touch the gasoline tax. Every other tax base—that is, every other tax other than tobacco, alcohol, and gasoline—is really small.

So in summary: we needed more revenue. We could raise fees, and we did, but they were a drop in the bucket. Tolls were out. Of all the tax bases, only income tax and sales tax were large enough to produce serious money.

Lots of people said we should have higher income taxes on the rich. The reality, unfortunately, is that Nova Scotia doesn't have enough rich people. We already have the most steeply progressive income tax in the country, and a new bracket wouldn't produce the revenue we needed. And the rich, of course, know better than anyone how to move their money around to avoid taxes.

Sales tax was the best option. Economists recommended it. The public preferred it. Wherever I went on the Back to Balance tour, I would put the income tax/sales tax choice to the room, and the consensus was always for sales tax (except in Amherst, because of the fear of cross-border shopping). Everyone agreed there should be a sales tax credit for people with modest incomes. But with that caveat, the consensus was clear that the HST was where we should look if we needed more revenue.

But What About Darrell's Promise?

The promise was made on May 19, 2009. During a televised leaders' debate on CBC, Darrell said, "We're not going to raise taxes." He could not have been more clear. Everybody saw it. Everybody heard it.

When you're on the campaign trail, there's no room for nuanced explanation of policy or even for hesitation. Kim Campbell, prime minister for four months in 1993, once famously said, "An election is no time to discuss serious issues." She was criticized for it, but every politician knows she was right.

The political need for crisp, clear answers is especially true when you're talking about an issue on which the voters have doubts. The NDP is stuck with the stereotype of being tax-huggers. Darrell had to confront that stereotype, so he said, "We're not going to raise taxes." It was the reassurance that voters needed. After the CBC debate, Darrell moved on and the voters moved on, but the bomb was planted. This promise was the second thing—MLA expenses being the other—that was already done when we walked across the Holiday Inn stage on election night of 2009 and that ended up undoing our government.

I know why Darrell said what he said. In his shoes, I would have said the same thing. But I was the finance critic for the NDP and most likely to be finance minister, and I was worried.

When we came into office, revenue wasn't even standing still—it was actually dropping. The economy was soft, and so income tax and sales tax revenue were correspondingly soft. Most importantly, revenue from oil and gas royalties fell precipitously. The Conservative government enjoyed royalty revenue of $452 million in their last year in office. That had dropped to $110 million in our first year, and by the end of our mandate petroleum royalties were essentially gone.

This loss of royalty revenue would, all by itself, have justified an HST increase. The health and education systems, as well as community services and transportation, needed the same revenue just to keep going as they were. You can't lose $342 million in royalty revenue and just shrug your shoulders and say, "We'll have to tighten our belts." It's impossible.

Besides, the Conservatives had made new operational spending commitments, even though they knew—or should have known—that petroleum royalties were about to head drastically downwards. The family pharmacare program, for example, was introduced in the dying days of the MacDonald government. It was a noble idea with a knuckle-whitening price tag. The only reason we can afford it at all, even today, is that not everybody who is eligible knows about it. If they signed up, it would immediately add tens of millions of dollars to provincial expenditure in an area where costs historically rise much faster than inflation or revenue. So we came to the conclusion that, promise or no promise, we had to raise more revenue through taxes.

The Choice We Made: Raising the HST

I can no longer remember exactly where or when or by whom the idea of raising the HST by 2 percent was first brought up. I think it was in a Department of Finance options paper, delivered to me shortly after taking office. They knew we needed more revenue, they knew what the options were, and they laid them out. Campaign promise? Not their problem.

When the HST came into effect in Nova Scotia on April 1, 1997, the Savage Liberals had set it at 15 percent. To the public, this headline number is all that matters. To governments, it mattered very much that the revenue was divided by sending 7 percent to the federal government and 8 percent to the provincial government.

The Harper Conservatives pledged in 2006 that they would reduce the HST by two percentage points, and when they were elected, they did. The federal share went down by 1 percent on July 1, 2006, and by another 1 percent on January 1, 2008, for a total at the cash register of 13 percent. The provincial government was still taking 8 percent, and the federal government was taking the other 5 percent.

Because of the cut in the federal share, we believed there was slack we could pick up to solve our revenue problem. If we increased the HST to 15 percent—or to be more precise, if we increased the provincial share of the HST by two percentage points to 10 percent—we would be returning the consumer total to the level it had been at between 1997 and 2006. At one point I proposed that we consider an increase to 16 percent, but Darrell rejected that out of hand as soon as he heard it. Nobody had complained much about the 15 percent rate, so it seemed reasonable to put it back up there, but not beyond.

In my budget speech on April 6, 2010, I announced an increase in the HST from 13 percent to 15 percent, along with a suite of related measures:

- removing the provincial portion of the HST from children's clothing and footwear, feminine hygiene products, and diapers;
- establishing the affordable living tax credit to cushion or eliminate the impact of the HST increase for households with an income below $30,000;
- establishing a poverty reduction credit to give $200 per year to about 15,000 low-income individuals;
- ensuring a refund of provincial income tax to any senior receiving the guaranteed income supplement; and
- increasing the income tax rate for those earning the most.

I also committed to keeping provincial HST off home heating and reducing the tax rate for small businesses.

This was a complex package of revenue measures. But like an elephant at a dance, the HST increase crowded everything else off the floor. If we had hoped to get some credit for the small-business tax reduction or the refund of income tax to low-income earners or taking the provincial HST off children's clothing, it didn't work.

Here's another thing we got no credit for: the affordable living tax credit returned $70 million to low-income households. It was explicitly designed to *more* than compensate those households for the HST increase, by about $20 million. They would end up with more money than they had before. Combined with the $31 million of income tax revenue from the new top tax bracket, this was as close to Robin Hood—take from the rich, give to the poor—as a modern government can get. But we didn't make a big splash out of it, and so our own people—the anti-poverty activists and even some of our own MLAS—missed what we were doing.

The main resistance to the HST increase wasn't about the rate but from the fact that we would now be out of step with other provinces. This was particularly true along the New Brunswick border, and I heard plenty about that during my stop in Amherst on the Back to

Balance tour. Merchants there were already struggling with cross-border shopping—a fact of life for decades in Amherst, given that Moncton is much closer than Halifax—and they feared that a 2 percent difference in sales tax would hasten the consumer exodus. I spent a great deal of time in Cumberland County in 2010 and 2011, gathering information, listening to people, and generally smoothing the waters. In the end, the HST increase didn't seem to have much impact one way or the other on cross-border shopping.

The Harper Conservatives knew that cutting the HST was bad economics but good politics. Every time someone went to the cash register, even for their daily coffee, they would be paying less. After we raised the HST, those same coffee-drinkers would be paying more, every day, and remembering that Darrell Dexter had broken his promise. Every. Day.

COULD WE LOWER THE HST?

The HST issue always troubled Darrell. He is an honourable person, and it troubled him that he had made a promise, even in the heat of an election campaign, that he did not keep.

At first, Darrell's defense to the broken promise was that the promise was not, in fact, in the official NDP election platform. When I first heard him say this, I was incredulous. Everyone remembered his making the promise. The words had come out of his mouth. How could he expect people to buy a hair-splitting distinction between what he said on province-wide television and what is in a platform document that only a handful of people had read? I told him, sitting beside him in the legislature, that this line of argument was a non-starter. But he persisted with it for too long.

Eventually, he came around to the idea that the HST had to come down, if for no other reason than to mitigate the damage of the broken promise. But was it really possible to drop the HST? Darrell certainly hoped so. He wanted to be able to say that the NDP raised the

HST only for as long as it was needed to balance the budget. The only question was when it would come down.

We had agreed, as far back as 2009, that the 2012 budget would lay the groundwork for the election expected in 2013. An election-year budget is too late and tends not to be taken seriously anyway. So as we moved towards the 2012 budget, the possibility of dropping the HST back to 13 percent was definitely on the table.

In the several months leading up to the 2012 budget, finance staff were bringing me figures that looked reasonably rosy, to the point where there was very serious internal discussion about cutting the HST in the 2012 budget. Unfortunately, the numbers started heading south starting about six weeks before the budget. I still don't know why. There were some frank discussions between me and staff. It appears that the original numbers had not been terribly realistic, especially on the expenditure side, and as the numbers got more refined as budget day approached, the room that we thought we had disappeared.

So we could not actually reduce the HST in 2012. The question remained: What were we going to say about the future of the HST? There was still definitely some room in future years, but only if we continued with tight expenditure control. In the end, we concluded it could be done. The HST would go down by one point in 2014 and by another in 2015.

After I resigned as finance minister, there was speculation that I had resigned over the HST-reduction promise. It's true there wasn't universal support within the NDP for bringing down the HST. Politicians—and I mean all politicians, not just in the NDP—can always figure out how to spend more money. But I supported the promise to reduce the HST. I wouldn't have delivered the budget if I hadn't agreed with it. When I told Darrell, three weeks later, that I was resigning as his finance minister, it wasn't over the HST.

10

RESIGNING AS THE MINISTER OF FINANCE

When you're in politics, you're supposed to want to be in Cabinet. Politicians put up with a lot in order to be *considered* for Cabinet. And yet on May 30, 2012, I resigned as finance minister. Nobody forced me out. Darrell asked me to stay, twice. But I left. I gave an explanation at the time, but many people thought there had to be another explanation. Somebody like me isn't supposed to just walk away.

Everything I said on the day I resigned was true. But yes, there was more.

Like most things in politics, the reasons were complex. There wasn't just one reason. There was a long list of reasons. I gave some of them on the day I resigned, but there were others. In particular, there was the last straw about which I have not spoken publicly until now.

SAME OLD, SAME OLD

If the primary motivation of every politician is to be re-elected—and it is—then thoughts of the next election are never far from the politician's mind.

In my first three elections—2001, 2003, 2006—there was never any question about whether I would be a candidate, so my thoughts were all about the details of the campaign. By 2009, I had gotten to the point of thinking about my exit from politics. I told my wife that, if we didn't win this time, it would be my last term. By the spring of 2012, I was again thinking about my political future. You might think it was an easy decision, now that we were finally in government, but it wasn't.

On the plus side, I was in the legislature, I was a Cabinet minister, I had a prominent role in the Dexter government. The job took me places and allowed me to do things that no other job could.

But I had plenty of doubts.

I had disdained professional politicians when I got into politics. I desperately didn't want to be one myself, but I knew I was almost there. One more election, and my chances of ever doing anything else were slim. There was already little chance of returning to law. I hadn't practiced full-time for fifteen years, and the law had changed under my feet. No law firm is interested in hiring someone with rusty skills and no clients. And it's precisely at this point—when the politician has no viable career alternatives other than staying in politics—that politicians become truly dangerous. If I were going to get out, it had to be soon.

Here's the problem: the skills and experience you gain as an MLA prepare you for nothing.

If you're a Cabinet minister, most of the real work—the work that has value in the job market—is done by civil servants. If you're an MLA, most of your time is spent doing constituency work—which has no value in the job market. If you can't go back to exactly what you were doing before, what do you have to offer? That's why so many ex-MLAS, including Cabinet ministers and premiers, struggle to find work after they resign, retire from politics, or get voted out.

I also had to be frank about the possibility we would lose the election. After you've been a Cabinet minister, the thought of going to the opposition benches is unbearable. I didn't want to be one of those politicians who ran, and won, and then resigned shortly afterwards just because they ended up on the opposition side. I had watched a number of others do it—the most memorable being Don Cameron in 1993, when he announced to his supporters, and the provincial television audience, that he was resigning the seat he'd won only minutes before—and it wasn't something to admire. If I wasn't prepared to serve a full term, no matter the outcome, I shouldn't re-offer.

I was no longer enjoying the constituency work. Given the centrality of constituency work to an MLA's life, that's a big confession. At the start, I had gotten a real charge out of solving someone's problem. Now, my assistant Cath Joudrey was doing most of the casework anyway, since I was a Cabinet minister and had less time to spend in the constituency office. The cases that came to me were the most intractable ones, and it had been a long time since I'd scored a satisfying win.

Then there were the usual stresses and strains of being in office. The Dexter government was unpopular, and it showed in every interaction we had. When a government is on the ropes, the tone changes—the tone of conversations and correspondence from the public, the tone of the opposition, the tone of news reports. I had watched it happen to other governments, and now it was happening to us. I was swimming in a sea of negativity, and it was wearing me down.

My health was getting worse. It was nothing specific, only the predictable result of failing to exercise and eat and sleep properly. When I looked around the Cabinet table, I saw—with the exception of Ross Landry, who always took his fitness seriously—a bunch of people who did not look well. I was sitting beside Paul MacEwan in 2002 when he suffered a brain aneurysm in the House. He was never the same again. I watched Eileen O'Connell and Michael Baker get sick and die in office. It's not worth being a politician if you have to trade it for your health.

So I was already in a bit of a funk when the House reconvened for the spring 2012 sitting. Two things happened in that spring sitting that tipped me over the edge.

The first was a simple question in question period. The question wasn't directed at me, and there was nothing unusual about it. I've looked through Hansard and can't pinpoint the exact day or the exact question. There are several possibilities. The point was the feeling it triggered in me, rather than the question itself. To understand the feeling, I have to give some background.

Electricity rates were always a significant issue during my time in the legislature. When we were in opposition, we hit on the idea of taking the provincial portion of the HST off home heat. This was a pocketbook issue that resonated with anyone who paid a power bill. The Conservatives first resisted, then took the tax off, then put it back on. It was easy for us to promise, in the 2009 election, that we would take the tax off and keep it off.

We didn't get much credit for taking the tax off electricity bills. There was general discontent over the fact that we'd increased the HST. Besides, any savings for ratepayers was quickly swallowed up by a series of rate increases that took power bills higher than they'd ever been. People were upset. Naturally the opposition parties blamed the government for these increases, and it was frequently raised in the legislature.

Sitting on the government side, I knew that the government's influence on Nova Scotia Power was a lot weaker than the opposition wanted the public to believe. It is, after all, a private company, regulated by an arm's-length tribunal, the Utility and Review Board, over which the government had zero day-to-day control.

More importantly, power rates are, at bottom, a simple process of adding up the cost of producing power and then dividing it fairly among the users. Of course there are plenty of technical details about how exactly to calculate the cost of power and how precisely to divide it up fairly. But the basic idea is adding up the cost and dividing it among the users. There are no magic answers.

The real issue with Nova Scotia's power rates is that most of our power production comes from particular kinds of fossil fuels. The price of those fuels is set on the international market, and so if we're going to have power, we have to pay that price. The challenge is to find a way to transfer our energy production from expensive and polluting fossil fuels to clean, stable sources. There is no magic answer here either. Wrong decisions are paid for over decades. Careless interference can be punished with rising rates, even brownouts and blackouts.

But in the legislature, you'd never know it. If you listen to the opposition, you would think that everything that happens on power rates is the fault of the government of the day—it isn't—and that there are simple solutions that will quickly bring down power rates—there aren't. The real issues are hard, but we hadn't acknowledged that when we were in opposition, and our opposition wasn't acknowledging it now.

I distinctly remember sitting in the House one day, watching Stephen McNeil ask about power rates during question period, and I was struck by how very much he sounded like Darrell Dexter when Darrell was on the other side of the House. Stephen was using the same words, the same tactics, and the same arguments that Darrell had used. And Darrell was giving the same replies that the Conservatives had given to him when he was the one posing the questions.

It struck me then, forcefully, that there was hardly any point to who sat in my chair or who was on which side of the House. None of us was dealing with the real issues. There was no fundamental difference between us. We were playing out a political charade, where our actions and reactions were dictated by our roles. I looked around the chamber, as if I were seeing it for the first time, and finally understood the futility of partisan politics.

Why accept a deterioration in my physical health, and the stress, and the time away from family, when it really made no difference whether I was there or not? The political charade, in which I had been a full participant for fourteen years, could carry on without me. That was my moment of revelation.

And then came the last straw.

WHEN I DECIDED TO RESIGN

The largest single expenditure of the government, by far, is the cost of people—wages, benefits, pensions. The provincial budget will stand or fall on how well it manages its people costs.

In the spring of 2012, we were on a collision course with the NSGEU. They had accepted, quickly and quietly, the first two years of 1 percent wage settlements, but now those agreements were coming to an end. Because the first settlement would establish a pattern for everyone else, they were very careful about which unit would go to the bargaining table first. We seemed curiously unable to match them strategically. We were dancing with people who knew all the moves, and we seemed compelled to follow their lead. The NSGEU chose Local 42, the health care bargaining unit in the Capital District Health Authority.

Let's be clear about why the NSGEU led with Local 42: That local would, if it went on strike, have the greatest and fastest impact on the greatest number of sick people. The thought process behind the union's choice disturbed me then and disturbs me now, but this is what passes for normal in public-sector collective bargaining.

On March 19th, Local 42 voted in favour of strike action. The CDHA put a strike plan in place. As the clock wound down toward the strike deadline, the CDHA had to cancel appointments and surgeries and emptied its large hospitals. The workers were still going to work, but there was less and less for them to do. Effectively, the bargaining unit was on strike, but they were going to work and being paid. In only a couple of days, hundreds or even thousands of sick Nova Scotians, and their families, were adversely affected.

Although there had been plenty of collective bargaining during our time in office, my involvement had been limited to what came before the Treasury Board. The heavy lifting was generally done by Shawn Fuller and Matt Hebb from the Premier's Office, and by Gordon Maclean from the Public Service Commission.

For reasons that were never explained to me, I was included in all the strategy calls on the NSGEU Local 42 negotiations. I had never been included at this level before. Over the course of about two weeks, I participated in at least half a dozen calls. The participants were me, Frank Corbett, Dan O'Connor, Shawn Fuller, Matt Hebb, and Gordon Maclean, and sometimes Rick Anderson from the Department of Health. So I had a ringside seat as events unfolded.

Early on, it was apparent that the union wasn't interested in a real deal. Their starting position for a three-year settlement was 5.1 percent plus inflation. A 5.1 percent wage demand, in the midst of an economic recession and stagnant public revenue, is not a serious proposal. Two additional years of inflation indexing had the potential to put the total settlement over 10 percent.

One of our first requests to the NSGEU was for them to give a definite number for the second and third year. The numbers that came back were large. I don't remember exactly what they were, but they were both over 3 percent. Inflation had been 3.8 percent in 2011, due to a big bump in food and energy prices, and that was all the justification the NSGEU needed. As finance minister I knew that big number would probably not be repeated—and as a matter of fact, subsequent inflation has been very low.

As the strike deadline loomed, and with the NSGEU intransigent in its demands, we prepared to introduce legislation to forestall the strike. On the day the legislation was to be introduced, Darrell met with our caucus. He was at his best. He was determined and articulate. With one exception—Howard Epstein—the caucus was united behind him. The caucus understood that legislative action was needed, and they were ready. Even Howard was willing to absent himself from the House rather than vote against the bill.

As I was leaving the caucus meeting through the back door, Shawn stopped me. He asked what I thought of a proposal that would include arbitration, with the employer's offer as a floor and the union's offer as a ceiling. The proposal also included several sweeteners.

The same proposal had been floated before, on our phone calls, and rejected. There was nothing new. I told Shawn, firmly, that I did not agree with the proposal. I reminded him that, throughout the process, I had been concerned about keeping the employer's offer on an all-in basis. The Treasury Board had approved a net offer of 2.0 percent–2.0 percent–2.9 percent. I told him that I was already concerned about whether the public would support this offer, which I considered to be generous and which would stretch the public's ability to pay. I doubted the public would support an offer where the floor was higher and an arbitration award might take it higher still.

When I left the building, I believed that things would unfold as Darrell had laid them out at the caucus meeting. Halfway through question period, the premier would invite the two opposition leaders to his office and show them the legislation that would be introduced. If the opposition leaders agreed, the bill could be introduced and passed that afternoon. Even if there was a delay, it wouldn't be for more than a couple of weeks, and the impact of the strike would lie firmly on the head of the opposition leader causing the delay.

I sat in the House and watched the plan unfold. Darrell did leave halfway through question period. Shortly afterwards, the two opposition leaders left.

Meanwhile, I was emailing with my wife about picking our son up from school. I was worried that I might not be able to get my car out of the Province House parking lot if the NSGEU descended on the legislature en masse. Although walking from school to the legislature was one of our pickup options, I suggested that he not come down to Province House. I didn't want my son walking into a crowd of angry union members.

We were ready. I was ready.

I stepped into the back room. I asked Frank Corbett, who had been over to the Premier's Office, what was happening. He said, "There's another proposal on the table." It was exactly the same proposal that Shawn had floated to me on my way out of the caucus meeting. It had been rejected on our phone calls. I had specifically rejected it, again, after the caucus meeting. And here it was, back on the table, except this time it was at the premier's table.

I knew what this meant. Darrell's staff had kept working on him after the caucus meeting, and they'd persuaded him that this alternative proposal would get the deal. There had been no consultation with the Treasury Board. There had been no consultation with the caucus about why the game plan had changed, even though Darrell had left the caucus meeting with strong support for the legislative option. The boys in the Premier's Office had gone to work on Darrell, and they didn't care what anybody else thought. Once the offer was made to the union, it couldn't be pulled back. And the premier had told his boys to make the offer.

I walked into the House. When I sat down, I turned to Maureen MacDonald and said, "They've just thrown in the towel."

At this point, I knew my time in Cabinet was over. All that was left was to work out the details.

HOW AND WHEN I RESIGNED

The tentative settlement with Local 42 happened on April 25, 2012. That was a Wednesday. (It was confirmed, after a union vote, two days later.)

I thought about it and thought about it for the rest of the week and over the weekend. Resigning from Cabinet is not something to be done lightly.

The problem was that the deal would put financial handcuffs on the government for years. There was no principled way to make one settlement with Local 42 and a different, lower settlement with other bargaining units.

The strains of governing in a recession were made bearable only by looking ahead to the payoff. This settlement meant there would be no payoff. All those hours spent in Treasury Board in the windowless, soulless Cabinet room were for nothing. The savings, and then some, were being handed over to public sector unions. I looked ahead and saw nothing that wasn't bleak. It didn't matter which party was in government. It didn't matter who was in the finance minister's chair. I couldn't stay.

The following Monday, I asked to speak with Darrell when I saw him at Province House, and we walked downstairs to a small meeting room. I told him I was going to resign as finance minister. I also told him that I thought Maureen would resign too. She and I had gone as far as talking about holding a joint news conference later that week. The first words out of his mouth were "This is going to kill us." I told him that my mind was absolutely made up. There was no chance of my staying on.

When he left, evidently to go across the street to his office, he must have spoken with at least some of his staff. Very shortly afterwards, Shawn asked to speak with me. I went with him down to the same room where I'd spoken with Darrell. He said that if I agreed to stay, he would resign instead. I told him that didn't make sense. I had decided to leave because I no longer believed in the government's fiscal plan. Having him leave would only make things worse. It wasn't a trade.

By coincidence, on the very same day that I told Darrell I was going to resign, I was scheduled to make my second-reading speech on the Financial Measures Act, which is part of the budget. I slashed the portions of the prepared text dealing with my confidence in the province's finances. I no longer believed it, so I couldn't say it.

Over the weekend I had written a script for my resignation announcement. I intended to deliver it that Thursday or maybe Friday. Meanwhile, though, Maureen was backing away from her own resignation. She seemed to feel too compromised to stay as health minister, and when she saw that I was determined to resign as finance minister, I think she saw an opportunity to get out of the Department of Health but stay in Cabinet. Her reasons for staying are for her to share, not me, but they did affect my own decision about how to resign. I decided an immediate resignation would do more harm than good, and it was never my intention to harm the Dexter government. The script I had written was never delivered.[1]

In order to minimize the damage, I agreed to stay on until the end of the legislative sitting. The next several weeks were painful. I knew I was leaving, but few others did. It was hard for me to work on issues with more than a short-term impact, because the thought in my head was *This will have to wait for the new minister.* I told my executive assistant, the deputy minister, the chair and CEO of the Nova Scotia Liquor Corporation, and the CEO of the Nova Scotia Pension Agency, but that's all.

Mentally I was already gone, but still I hung on until Darrell was ready. The House finished on May 17th. I called Dan O'Connor one day, around that time, and told him how difficult it was for me to continue and that I just wanted to get it over with. At this point he mentioned that Bill Estabrooks would be stepping down as well. Bill, who had let it be known the previous year that he was suffering from Parkinson's, had received medical advice that he needed a less demanding role. Both Dan and I recognized that having more than one minister step down provided convenient cover.

Finally the appointed day arrived. It was Wednesday, May 30, 2012. I had signed the resignation letter the day before, in Darrell's office. It's very easy to resign. The executive council office has had lots of practice preparing resignation letters. It's one sentence.

That afternoon, as I looked on, Maureen MacDonald was sworn in as Nova Scotia's new finance minister. I walked alone out of Government House, down Barrington Street toward Province House to get my car and drive away.

I was a backbencher, and I was free.

---

1   See Appendix 1, "The News Conference I Never Held."

11

RETURNING TO CABINET

WHY I CAME BACK

was a backbencher, and I was bored.

If there's a political role worse than being a government back-bencher, I don't know what it is. All the decisions are made by other people, but you have to defend them as if you made them yourself.

In the House, I sat behind Ross Landry at the end of the second row. I generally detested the foolishness of question period and often didn't attend. I did attend on March 27, 2013, and was perplexed by how bad Darrell was. I think this struck me particularly because the questions were about the auditor general's comment that $27 million should have been added to the provincial deficit in the last budget that I delivered. The opposition was coming at Darrell with partisan, rhetorical questions (like "How can Nova Scotians trust his government ever again?"). Darrell's tone was flat and his responses were bureaucratic ("The revenue estimates that came in after the posted date for the budget were in fact corrected, and they were corrected in the first financial forecast update.").

I went up to Darrell's office afterwards and asked to see him. I told him his performance in the House had been painfully bad. I told him he wasn't being well supported by his staff if he could go into the House so ill-prepared. I told him we had to face the fact that his name and his image were in bad shape.

Darrell's reply was intended to be reassuring but wasn't: "Things are going fine. I don't know what you're talking about." He mentioned his recent weight loss and how he hadn't felt this good in a long time. I left his office shaking my head, knowing that I'd been talking to a premier who was sleepwalking to electoral disaster. Were his staff shielding him from the truth? Was he shielding himself from the truth?

Mentally I was already out of politics. As time went on, still with no election call—and with speculation the election might be put off until the spring of 2014—I contacted the Speaker's Office about resigning my seat at the end of August 2013. I needed to get on with my life.

And then, suddenly, I was back in Cabinet.

On May 9, 2013, the House went in at noon. As usual, I missed most of question period but did go in toward the end. When I stepped out again, after question period had ended, Percy Paris was in the back room with a few others. They seemed to be comforting him, which was odd, but I didn't stay to find out what was going on.

Sometime over the course of the afternoon, I heard there had been an incident in the washroom, just after question period, involving Percy and Keith Colwell, the Liberal member for Preston. Later that afternoon I was outside the library and watched a scrum involving Allan McMaster, the Conservative member for Inverness. He'd seen the incident and was taking reporters through what he'd seen. I called the Premier's Office to say that we really should have someone over at Province House to monitor what was being said.

By the time I got home that afternoon, I knew enough to say to my wife, "Percy's going to have to resign." As the evening progressed, and as I thought about the political logic of the situation, I thought about calling Darrell to let him know that I would be willing to step in to help.

Why did I think of volunteering to step back into Cabinet? I was bored as a backbencher, but there was more to it than that. I had resigned from Cabinet, but I still supported Darrell and the government. If that were not true, I would have left the NDP caucus and I would have voted against the 2013–14 budget. This distinction, between supporting a government in general but disagreeing on a specific issue, can be difficult to grasp, but to me it's fundamental. I believed then, and believed up to the day I cast my vote in the 2013 election, that re-electing Darrell Dexter and the NDP was the best choice for Nova Scotians.

So I thought about calling Darrell, but didn't. When my phone rang later that evening, I knew who it would be and why he was calling. Darrell told me that Percy was going to resign. Percy had gone to the police station alone, without legal advice, and the police were going to charge him on the strength of his own account of what happened. Darrell asked me if I would rejoin his Cabinet.

Because I'd already thought it through before Darrell called, I agreed immediately. The next morning, there was a caucus meeting in the Cabinet room at One Government Place. Darrell informed the caucus that Percy had resigned and that I would be returning to Cabinet.

I was sworn in at 9:30 that morning, in the seventh floor meeting room at One Government Place. Maureen was also there, since she would be taking on African Nova Scotian Affairs. We were sworn in by chief justice Michael MacDonald. The contrast with my first Cabinet swearing-in could not have been more stark. My first swearing-in, back in June 2009, had been in front of a large crowd of family, friends, and supporters at the Cunard Centre, with the good will of the crowd radiating onto the stage. My second swearing-in, to the Cabinet of a government on the edge of extinction, was in front of half a dozen people in the premier's conference room. It took about five minutes.

WHAT I SAW WHEN I GOT THERE

My time as minister of ERDT, from May to October 2013, was the most interesting summer job I ever had. Just as the Department of Finance is connected, directly or indirectly, to every aspect of government operations, so ERDT is connected, directly or indirectly, to every aspect of Nova Scotia's economy. There was lots to do, and not much time to do it.

Concluding the Shipbuilding Deal

One big file that was still outstanding when I got to ERDT was the negotiation of the final agreement with Irving Shipbuilding Inc. (ISI).

On October 19, 2011, the federal government announced that ISI had been chosen to build Canada's new combat vessel fleet as part of the national shipbuilding procurement strategy. The contract's value was estimated at $25 billion and was expected to create 11,500 jobs and add almost $1 billion to Nova Scotia's economy each year during peak production. Darrell called it "a defining moment in Nova Scotia's history."

Part of the ISI bid was the promise of a financial contribution from the provincial government. It was an essential part of the bid, and we were certain that the contract would not be won by ISI without it. When the contract was awarded in October 2011, ISI and the provincial government—led by Paul Black from the Premier's Office—started negotiating the terms of the provincial assistance. A letter of offer was signed during the summer of 2012.

I had almost no personal involvement with the shipbuilding contract when I was the finance minister. The file was being run out of the Premier's Office with support from ERDT. When the letter of offer was presented to the Treasury Board for approval, it was treated by all concerned as a done deal.

Our government's role in winning the contract—the largest industrial contract in Nova Scotia's history—should have given us a political boost, but instead it turned into one of our biggest political liabilities. There was going to be a long wait between the awarding of the contract in 2011 and the time when shipbuilding actually started. The euphoria went flat. In this vacuum, the idea took firm hold among the public that the Dexter government's financial support was too rich—and why were we giving money to the Irvings anyway?

When I went to ERDT, I was surprised to learn that the deal still wasn't completely done. The letter of offer was essentially a high-level summary. The details were still being worked on when I arrived at ERDT and had reached a stalemate. One of my first meetings as ERDT minister was with Jim Irving and Darrell, and we agreed I would personally lead the provincial negotiating team.

The Irvings didn't get rich by being pushovers. There were many lengthy meetings over many weeks. We negotiated first with senior executives from ISI and then eventually with Jim Irving himself. He's a big fellow with a big personality. He did not immerse himself in the details—he left that to his executives—but he always had his eye on closing the deal.

From our perspective, we were trying to put flesh on the bones of the letter of offer that had been negotiated in mid-2012. We were having trouble because the ISI executives who had negotiated that letter of offer were gone, and ISI didn't seem to have a lot of corporate memory to draw on. The new ISI executives were essentially trying to negotiate the deal all over again—or at least that's how we saw it.

From the ISI perspective, they were pushing for terms of loan forgiveness that would be as quick and easy as possible. I pointed out to the ISI negotiators that the shipbuilding deal had turned into one of the biggest negatives for our government. The public would not stand for terms that were more generous to ISI than those that had already been announced.

We all knew an election was imminent, and ISI must have known it was better for them to finalize the deal rather than wait for the election result. We stood our ground, and ISI came around. We finalized the deal in early July. The documents were delivered to me for signature in the legislature on July 5th, when we held a special session to fend off the looming paramedics' strike. I leaned over to Darrell to show him the documents. Then I added my signature, and the shipbuilding deal was done.

We haven't heard the last of the shipbuilding deal. No matter what contract we sign, the Irvings will always push. That's how they do business. They'll come back, again and again, over the life of the deal, to push for better terms or a more favourable interpretation. Future governments will feel the pressure, and when they do, their inclination will be to follow the Rules of the Game, and blame the Dexter government for negotiating a bad deal. But the deal is a good one. As long as the federal government follows through with it, the shipbuilding contract really will be a defining moment in Nova Scotia's history.

Concluding the Ferry Deal

The other big file that was outstanding when I got to ERDT was the Yarmouth ferry.

I've already recounted how the decision was made to end the ferry subsidy, and the ensuing fallout. When I rejoined his Cabinet, Darrell asked me to pay particular attention to the southwest, and I understood that to mean that I should make the ferry file my top priority. I got to know the highway between Halifax and Yarmouth well.

By May 2013, efforts were well under way to restore a ferry service. The first call for proposals hadn't succeeded. The department learned from that false start, and the second call for proposals was supported by a determined effort to get out and beat the bushes for likely operators. A group of leading Yarmouth citizens and municipal leaders, known as the International Ferry Partnership, was working closely with the government. The co-chairs were Keith Condon, one of the owners of Yarmouth-based Tri-Star Industries, and Neil LeBlanc, the former Conservative MLA, finance minister, and Consul General to New England. Keith, in particular, played a remarkable role. He is a successful business owner with an unerring nose for the deal, and he doesn't let emotions or personalities—or politicians—get in the way.

So my job, really, was to keep the process moving, clear any road-blocks, and otherwise just get out of the way.

The deadline for submissions was June 20th, later extended to July 4th. Although the department had been working with several opera-tors, we didn't know for sure whether they would submit a proposal. In fact, the day before the deadline we had two news releases pre-pared—the first said we were pleased to have submissions and out-lining the next steps, and the second said we were disappointed that no submissions had been received. In the end, thankfully, we were able to use the first one. Three submissions came in. Two were from experienced operators—Balearia and P&O Ferries—and the third was from a new consortium called STM Quest.

In the end, after careful review, we went with STM Quest. They had the best ship—a new ferry that was sitting unused in Singapore—but had the least amount of operating experience. We appointed a team, led by David Oxner of the Gateway Secretariat, to negotiate the details. I gave them three weeks. It took the whole three weeks, and at least a couple of times it looked like it wasn't going to happen, but finally the deal was done. I had asked that some of the negotiating be done in Yarmouth, and I was pleased that the handshakes happened at the Rodd Grand Hotel on Main Street in Yarmouth. I announced the ferry deal on CJLS Radio in Yarmouth on Thursday, September 5th.

The election was called two days later. Of course there were accu-sations, before and after, that the deal was done only because the elec-tion was imminent, but that's not true. The search for a new operator was well under way when I got to ERDT. I pushed it along because it needed to be pushed. The deal had to be done by September so that marketing could start for the 2014 season. The negotiations took exactly the time they needed, no more and no less. I never had a conversation with Darrell, or anyone else, about linking the ferry announcement and the election call.

There was one more quirk about the ferry deal. There were a number of conditions that STM Quest had to meet before provincial money would flow. Normally the deal would have been signed there in Yarmouth and STM Quest would have gotten busy fulfilling the conditions. They took the peculiar position, though, that they would fulfill the conditions and *then* they would sign the deal. And so, as a matter of fact, the deal was signed by the new Liberal government, not by us.

There are plenty of things that could still go wrong with the ferry. It will always be a tough service to make profitable. We can't fondly remember a different era and wish ourselves back there. But the operators we selected have a decent chance of making it work.

When we came into office, the economy of the southwest was in tough shape. In a fair world, the Conservatives and Liberals would be held accountable for their contribution to the southwest's problems. But instead, we cut the ferry subsidy and made ourselves the scapegoat for every problem in the region. If the new ferry succeeds, everybody will claim a piece of the credit and the Liberals will say it was their deal. If the new ferry fails again, even many years in the future, you know who will be blamed.

That's politics. Those are the Rules of the Game.

12

THE END

Y ou could say that it was my signature that killed the Dexter government.

An election is called with an order in council, and it takes five signatures for an order in council to be valid. The OIC for the 2013 election was prepared and then walked around by Jeannine Lagasse, secretary of the executive council, to get the signatures. I was, on the afternoon of Friday, September 6, 2013, the fifth and final minister to sign the order in council dissolving the House and setting the date of the election. I signed it in Jeannine's office, around 4:00 P.M., then headed over to the Old Triangle pub to celebrate with ERDT staff the previous day's ferry announcement.

With my signature, the order in council was ready to go to the Lieutenant-Governor. The House of Assembly was dissolved, the election was on, and the Dexter government was done.

WHAT WENT WRONG?

The Dexter government did plenty of good things. But it has not been my purpose in writing this book to praise the Dexter government, nor to condemn it. My purpose in writing this book has been to look at the political culture that formed the background to the rise and collapse of the Dexter government. Others can assess the Dexter government's policy record better, and more objectively, than I can.

On a strictly political level, the Dexter government was a failure. The election verdict of October 8, 2013, was final and conclusive.

There are three broad explanations for why the Dexter government failed politically.

The first is that the economy dragged us down and would have dragged down any other government. We came into office at the beginning of a global recession. We hoped in 2009 that the Nova Scotia economy would recover in time for the 2013 election, but it didn't. People were not feeling better off under the Dexter government, and it's a short step from there to blaming the government.

The truth is that it was never within our government's power to shield Nova Scotia from the recession. Nova Scotia is a tiny piece of the continental and global economy with limited natural resources and a dependence on imported fossil fuels for energy. A small change in interest rates or the US dollar exchange rate has more impact on the Nova Scotia economy than every combined tool available to the provincial government.

But everyone, the NDP included, long ago bought into the idea that the provincial government has a major impact on the economy. When we were in opposition, we blamed the government for any economic problems. When we were in government, we took credit for any economic successes. When the economy continued to drag through 2011 and 2012 and into 2013, we were caught in a trap that we'd set for ourselves. We couldn't escape the blame. If this first explanation—that we were dragged down by economic circumstances over which we had little control—is right, then we should stop right there. It's only the Rules of the Game that demand we go further. The Rules of the Game say that it has to be somebody's fault.

The second broad explanation for why the Dexter government failed politically is that we were not up to the job. I don't think it's right—we had about the same amount of intelligence and ability as any other government I've seen—but if you're already inclined to think this way it's not hard to marshal a case.

You could say that we spent so long working toward winning that we forgot why we wanted to win. After our victory in June 2009, we were essentially making it up as we went along. Since we no longer had real policy objectives, only electoral objectives, we were buffeted by events. And during a recession, there are plenty of events. The issues that ended up defining us—a shipbuilding contract, a ferry, a couple of pulp mills, and an expense scandal—weren't mentioned or even imagined during the 2009 campaign.

You could say that Darrell immersed himself in the wrong issues. If a premier is going to keep his head above water, he has to focus on a small number of winnable issues, own them, and get credit for good results. But the core priorities process, led by Rick Williams and the office of policy and priorities, essentially led nowhere and trickled out to nothing. The P & P committee of Cabinet stopped meeting, in favour of decision-making out of the Premier's Office. The Premier's Office, in turn, was consumed by the events of the day and lost sight of the big picture. So Darrell became immersed in, and defined by, events that he could not control and that he could not win.

You could say that our election in 2009 depended too much on Darrell's public image. The Darrell Dexter that voters thought they saw in the 2009 election is, in fact, the real Darrell Dexter. He really is affable and smart. He really is the guy you want to go for a beer with. But by the 2013 election voters had lost faith in him. His popularity in 2009 lifted the party up, and his unpopularity in 2013 dragged the party down.

You could say that Darrell was too loyal to the people—Dan, Shawn, Matt, and Paul—who were around him during the slow build from the time he took the party's leadership in 2001 to our election victory in 2009. Each, in his own way, brought experience and talent to the Premier's Office. But when the poll numbers started dropping, they all—Darrell included—seemed unwilling to face it and unable to respond.

There's a third explanation, and it is that we got so busy with governing that we forgot the Rules of the Game—like the fact that perception is reality. The reality is that provincial financial assistance was an essential element of the winning shipbuilding bid. The perception is we handed hundreds of millions of dollars to one of the richest families in Atlantic Canada. The reality is that we spent more per P–12 student than any previous government. The perception is we slashed education spending. The reality is that we took provincial sales tax off home heating. The perception is that we were too cozy with Nova Scotia Power.

The political jungle is governed by the Rules of the Game, but we started playing by the Laws of Finance. It was classic NDP—if only we could *explain* what we were doing and *educate* people, they would *understand*. Meanwhile our opponents kept playing by the Rules of the Game. We got our political heads handed to us on a platter.

Once you lose swing voters, it's really hard to get them back. We started losing them after the MLA expense scandal, and we kept losing them. At a certain point, we reached a critical mass of unpopularity, after which we got blamed for everything. I'd seen it happen to other governments, and I watched bemusedly as it happened to us. The Metro Transit strike in February 2012, for example, was laid at Darrell's door by riders who had to figure out how to get around in the middle of winter. Those were our people, and they were mad. They didn't care that transit is municipal. They didn't care that the NDP prefers resolutions to be negotiated, not imposed. They wanted Darrell to do something, and he didn't.

I don't know which of the three explanations is correct—maybe it was some combination of each—but it's much too early to predict which particular narrative will take hold.

The closest analogy to what happened to the Dexter government is the Savage Liberal government in 1993. Like us, it too came to office in the middle of a deep recession. Only six years later, it was all gone. John Savage resigned in 1997, having sunk to very low personal approval ratings. Time has been kinder to the Savage government, and to John Savage himself, and I expect something similar will happen with the Dexter government. Much depends on how some of the longer-term Dexter policy initiatives—for example, the shipbuilding contract, the Maritime Link, and the Yarmouth ferry—actually play out.

WHAT COMES NEXT?

The British politician Enoch Powell, in his biography of another British politician, wrote something which strikes at political ambition: "All political lives, unless they are cut off in midstream at a happy juncture, end in failure, because that is the nature of politics and of human affairs."

On the happy side, then, are those who choose to get out when they're in midstream, like Frank McKenna of New Brunswick or Gary Doer of Manitoba, both of whom resigned after ten years of premiership. For some, it is death in office that cuts them off in midstream, like Angus L. Macdonald or Michael Baker or the Kennedy brothers, though death seems a high price to pay for fond remembrance. Then there are the rest of us.

This is the dark side of politics, which doesn't get talked about as much as it should. Losing an election can be devastating, or seem so. You feel like your neighbours have rejected you, even though you have worked long and hard for them. *What was it all for?* you ask, and maybe your spouse and your kids ask it too. Being away from home so much can put irreparable strains on marriage and family. As Robert Chisholm said to me once, everybody's political career comes to an end, and when you go home at the end of it you want to be sure the ones you love are still there. Politicians are as subject as anyone to family troubles, to alcoholism and other addictions, to strains on physical and mental health. The hush-hush atmosphere that surrounds politicians' personal problems only makes it worse.

When you enter the fray, the message "all political lives end in failure" is not one you are ready to receive. When you win an election, you float on a cloud for months. You don't believe anything can touch you. And that's why failure, when it arrives, hits so hard and hurts so much. If only you knew it was coming, it would do less damage. If you knew it was coming, just not when, you would work like hell to get stuff done before it arrived.

When I resigned as finance minister I knew my political time was up. That's why I announced, at the same time I resigned from Cabinet, that I would not be a candidate in the next election.

I'm often asked if I'm thinking of running for Parliament or for the party leadership. Aren't those the natural next steps?

I'm not interested in federal politics for the simple reason that the factors driving me away from provincial politics are magnified at the federal level. Politics in the House of Commons is aggressively nasty. Life is too short to get mixed up in that kind of thuggery. I also don't want to be a party leader. I've seen many leaders come and go, in my party and in other parties, and I have a pretty good idea of what it takes. I don't have what it takes, and I'll spare Nova Scotians the ordeal of watching me prove it.

Even if I were thinking about re-engaging at some point, I would come with baggage. I have given the bad guys twelve years' worth of words as hostages. My time as finance minister, in all its political and economic complexity, will be reduced to one-liners ("he raised taxes," "he never balanced the budget," "he added a billion dollars to the debt"). Besides, merely being associated with the Dexter government will be enough to dismiss anything I have to say, at least for a while.

After twelve years in the legislature and fifteen years in daily politics, I need a break from politics, and politics needs a break from me.

I still believe in good public policy, but the best way for me to make a positive contribution to good public policy is to get out of politics.

WHERE IS POLITICS GOING?

I'm not keen on where our politics is headed. Starting in the United States, then moving into Canada at the federal level, politics has become a never-ending election campaign and a continuous marketing scheme. Modern politics haven't arrived in their full glory in Nova Scotia yet, but they're partly here, and the rest is coming soon enough.

Modern politics means you build a base of voters who will vote for you no matter what. You do whatever it takes to keep your base hungry and angry. If that means stoking resentment and creating division, you do it. You ignore anyone who isn't thinking of voting for you, except to suppress their vote. You market yourself to the waverers by figuring out what they want and then promising it to them. You don't just criticize your opponents, you demonize them. You don't just demonize them, you destroy them. You claim credit for yourself and blame for your opponents and then repeat those claims, over and over. You undermine the source of any facts or arguments that run counter to your claims. Attack, attack, attack. It's just politics.

Real governing—governing on behalf of all, governing by balancing interests, governing on the evidence—is hard. So in modern politics you govern to win the next election. Governing is fully subordinated to the politics of winning—but win for what? Why, to win, of course. You win to win. You win so the other guys don't win. You win not to lose. You win because you can. This is the way that politics and parties are going, and I have no place in it.

These days the individual politician has vanished almost to nothing. A really good constituency politician knew the district, knew the people, knew who the opinion leaders were. Nowadays the Big Data people know a riding better than any politician could. A politician says, "But the people in my constituency won't support that," and the Big Data guy says, "You're wrong, they do, or more importantly, the people in the 5 percent of your electorate that we're targeting with this policy do support it." The worst of it is that the Big Data guy is right. He's got better information.

The days are gone when a politician can legitimately claim to know his or her riding better than anyone else. That is a profound change in our politics, because that constituency input was the only reason left for prime ministers or premiers to listen to their caucus. In the new politics, the role of the constituency politician is to feed the party's database, which is used for ever more sophisticated marketing schemes. Our constituency politicians have less impact on governing than ever. That's why they focus so much on constituency work and bringing home government money for this project or that organization. What else is left for them to do? It's the only place where they get real, personal satisfaction. Their last hope is to be considered for a Cabinet post, because they imagine that Cabinet ministers, at least, have a say. But the new politics is heading toward the neutering of Cabinet ministers, too.

POLITICAL PARTIES

After fifteen years in daily politics, I am less a fan than I ever was of political parties. There isn't that much difference between the parties in Nova Scotia. That may not seem much of a revelation to the cynics, but it was a revelation to me. The set of reasonable, thoughtful, moderate responses to the policy issues confronting us is small. If political leaders were bowling pins, then all the leaders I've seen in Nova Scotia could be knocked over with one ball. There are differences between them in emphasis, but that's all. So I have come to believe that parties do more harm than good.

Frankly I have trouble explaining what ideological labels—like conservative, liberal, social democrat, what have you—have to do with everyday political decision-making. It is not conservatism that is going to help you decide how to handle an allegation of decades-old sexual and physical abuse at a public institution. It is not socialism that is going to help you decide whether there should be nine or four or two regional health authorities.

Besides, if constituency work is what most MLAS are doing most of the time—and it is—then party labels are irrelevant. There is no difference among the parties in their approach to constituency work. There are good constituency politicians, and bad ones, in every party.

Parties are supposed to supply predictability and stability to the political system. Without parties, the voter could vote for the best local candidate but wouldn't have any idea what to expect from the government. The problem with this theory is that we have parties, and the voter *still* doesn't have any idea what the government will do. Platforms are marketing documents. The parties manufacture differences for election purposes, then once they become government, they face the same challenges, options, and constraints as the last government, which leads to remarkably similar decisions.

An alternative path would be to promote more Independent candidates. I love the idea, if I were an Independent MLA, of listening to everyone and then making up my own mind on the issues of the day, in a way that makes the most sense for my constituents. I might be influenced by others, I might occasionally ally myself with others, I might tend to vote similarly to others, but the final decision on every vote would be mine, guided only by my conscience and my constituents. Sitting as an Independent would be liberating.

It is, unfortunately, formidably difficult for an Independent to be elected. Reaching out to voters takes plenty of time and money, and parties help to get the message out in a way that an Independent cannot. That's why very few people are elected as an Independent in Nova Scotia. Paul MacEwan and Billy Joe Maclean did it in the 1980s, but nobody has succeeded since. And MacEwan and Maclean were unique, colourful characters.

Here are a couple of other, more radical ideas.

What if we formed a government from the best people in the whole House? We're more likely to get the best Cabinet timber if the starting pool is fifty-one, rather than thirty-three (McNeil), thirty-one (Dexter), thirty or twenty-five (Hamm), twenty-three (MacDonald), or nineteen (MacLellan). A team of decent, hardworking, honest people, who are guided by the facts and open to vigorous but respectful debate, are worth more than all the partisans in the world. This system would encourage more Independents and more independent thinking.

But even a pool of fifty-one is too limited. What if only some of the Cabinet had to come from the House and the rest came from the best that Nova Scotia could offer? It's not an absolute constitutional requirement that ministers be elected to the House, although that's certainly the convention. But the premier and elected ministers could answer in the House for any unelected minister.

Yes, I know: these are crazy ideas, and there are plenty of other crazy ideas. But if I've learned one big thing from my time in politics, it is that the current way of doing things is not working to make life better for Nova Scotians. The parties invent differences between them. The House is a charade. Our politicians follow the Rules of the Game. The real issues are hard, and our current system allows our politicians to avoid dealing with them.

For the public good, something different has to be done. Something different has to be *tried*. We have to stop reaching for escape hatches and justifying the status quo. Otherwise, we'll just keep watching the same bad movie, over and over.

BETTER POLITICIANS?

I worry when I see bright-eyed new politicians. Politics is a low, dirty business, but they don't believe it, or they think to themselves "*I'm different. I'll rise above it.*" They've haven't learned yet that politics has chewed up and spat out people better, smarter, and tougher than them. By the time they figure that out, it's too late.

So we have a steady stream of new politicians, myself included, who get into politics with the best of intentions. But nobody is an exception to Enoch Powell's maxim that all political lives end in failure, because that is—as he said—the nature of politics and of human affairs. We ex-politicians look back, and it's hard to see our footprints in the sand. We thought we would make a difference. We didn't. We thought we were better than whoever we replaced. We weren't.

Sure, all politicians can list accomplishments. It's not possible to be in elected office and accomplish literally *nothing*. Every Nova Scotia government has control of billions of dollars. It has its fingers in a thousand pies. Every government is going to do *something* right, and in fact every government does a lot of things right. Even the politician who never makes it to government is going to do good work around the constituency. But what we ex-politicians don't want to admit is that someone else in the same seat would have done the same or similarly worthy things.

It's too easy to say we need better politicians. They don't exist, and the search itself can be dangerous because it's just another escape hatch, and it leaves us vulnerable to political charlatans.

The fact is that our politicians are us. There isn't a better, more perfect, more angelic version of us. The people who are elected to office used to be us, and once they're in office, they respond in human ways to the pressures of the job. You would do the same if you were elected.

Yes, you would.

And if you think you wouldn't, you'd be one of those bright-eyed politicians who didn't know what they were getting into.

ENGAGED CITIZENS

Our politics are in a bad way because politicians succeed by following the Rules of the Game, and the Rules of the Game are incompatible with good government. The Rules of the Game are stronger than anything else. They're stronger than common sense and civility. They're stronger than logic, arithmetic, and science. They're stronger than any values or principles that the new politician brings with him or her.

Politicians follow the Rules of the Game *because they work*. They work to win votes, and votes mean re-election. The Rules of the Game will change when they stop working. The only person who is in a position to make that happen is the individual voter—in a word: you.

Winston Churchill said, "At the bottom of all the tributes paid to democracy, is the little man, walking into the little booth, with a little pencil, making a little cross on a little bit of paper—No amount of rhetoric or voluminous discussion can possibly palliate the overwhelming importance of that point." With due allowance for the era in which he was speaking—we might prefer "person" instead of "man," and the technology of voting will change—Churchill was putting his finger on the basic miracle of democracy. The whole modern effort of politics is directed at influencing how "the little person" will vote. Everything—the invention of differences, the attention-grabbing rhetoric, the focus on scandal and personality, the refusal to deal with the real issues, the devaluing of legislative work in favour of constituency work, the selection of candidates, everything—is aimed at winning your vote. It's a permanent marketing campaign, not fundamentally different from the marketing campaign of a company trying to sell you laundry detergent.

There will always be people who buy a box of laundry detergent because it's what their parents used, because it's what they've always used, because a friend recommended it, because they like the colour of the box, because they like the ads, because there's a coupon—anything but what's actually in the box. They've used it before and it works well enough, and they have better things to do than to study the chemistry of laundry detergent.

Voters can be like that, too. For those who are open to voting more than one way, politics can be bewildering. The political marketers know that, and they want to make it simple.

The main difference between political marketing and consumer marketing is that consumer marketing has standards. There are, for example, truth-in-advertising rules that limit what the company can claim about its own product or say about its competitors' product. In politics, there are no standards and no limits. We can't control the political marketing message coming at us, but we can control how we react to it. If there is hope, it lies in the space between when the political message is received and when we react. The political marketers would like the reaction to be instant—in fact they depend on it—but it doesn't have to be instant.

There is a space between reception and reaction, and we can train ourselves first to recognize the space, then to control it. We can control it, for example, by learning about the marketing techniques that are being used on us; by finding reliable sources of information and analysis; and by spotting when our politicians are following the Rules of the Game or reaching for an escape hatch, and asking them to stop and get back to the real issues.

It is not our politicians who will lead the change. The only person who can change our politics is the engaged citizen.

THE END

And so I found myself in the CBC studio on election night.

The NDP had been trailing the Liberals in the polls since the middle of 2012, and by the beginning of the campaign, the Liberal lead was 10 percentage points. In order to make up that much ground during a campaign, the NDP would have had to come out with a focused, hard-hitting attack campaign, and the Liberals would have had to run a weak campaign and suffer some idiot eruptions.

Within a week, it became obvious that the NDP would be running a safe, middle-of-the-road campaign, and the Liberals would be smart and calm. Stephen McNeil and the Liberals campaigned on a platform that essentially consisted of not being Darrell Dexter and the NDP.

The Liberal lead widened.

I participated very little in the campaign. My main contribution was playing Stephen McNeil in the three leadership debate rehearsals with Darrell. I lacked McNeil's stature, but I found the role easy to play. Stephen McNeil takes a very traditional approach to politics. He plays by the Rules of the Game, and after fifteen years in the business, I know how to act the part.

By now, we all know the results of Election 2013. The Liberals won 45 percent of the vote, which is, coincidentally, the same share won by the NDP in 2009. This was good for thirty-three seats, including most of the Halifax Regional Municipality. The NDP sank to only seven seats. The Conservatives had a stronger showing than in 2009, though not by much—2 percent more vote and one more seat—but they benefitted from a sense of upward momentum, especially in contrast to the NDP debacle. The Conservatives formed the official opposition.

On September 7, 2013, with the issuing of the writ of election, I had ceased to be an MLA.

On October 22, 2013, with the swearing in of the new government, I ceased to be a Cabinet minister. I was out of politics for the first time in fifteen years.

And now that my political career has ended, I have finally learned enough about politics to get started.

THE NEWS CONFERENCE I NEVER HELD

This is the text of the statement that I drafted for my resignation announcement during the week of April 30, 2012. It has not been changed since the day I wrote it. After concluding that this way of proceeding would do more harm than good, I never delivered it.

Earlier today, I submitted to the premier my resignation from the Cabinet.

I will continue to serve as the MLA for Halifax Fairview.

As I understand the principle, a Cabinet minister who has misgivings about a major decision or policy direction of the government must resign.

I have resigned because I have misgivings about the policy direction of the government that is embodied in last week's contract settlement with the NSGEU.

This settlement, and the arbitration that flows from it, will now form the basis for all public service contract settlements covering the next three years.

To put it simply, I am not sure that the settlement is financially sustainable, no matter what the outcome of the arbitration.

And in the long run, this settlement will likely contribute to the weakening of important public services, including health care.

This is a complicated area. There are many complex factors in play. Reasonable people can easily come to different conclusions. When dealing with big public-policy issues, there is rarely a single "right" answer. But given my misgivings, my understanding is that I must step down as a Cabinet minister, and so that is what I have done.

I can't possibly explain, in detail, all of the thought process behind my decision. I believe that at least some of what happened over the past couple of weeks falls under Cabinet confidentiality, which I take very seriously, and so I find myself in the peculiar position of resigning from Cabinet without being able to explain exactly why.

I did, however, note an interview done on CBC Radio last week with Mary Jane Hampton, a Halifax-based health care consultant, and I agree with and adopt everything she said.

For today's purposes, let me try to summarize my decision with two thoughts.

The first is that by far the largest part of the government's expenses is wages and related items such as pensions and benefits. If we take all of the limited new money we have and spend it on higher wages and benefits, all we're doing is buying more of the same. We are not investing in more innovation, greater efficiency, higher productivity, better services, or better health outcomes for Nova Scotians. None of these things was on the table during the negotiations.

My second thought is simply that the province's finances are not yet in a position to sustain public-sector wage settlements of this size.

I'm not suggesting that bad things will happen next week, next month, or even next year. The health care system will probably carry on much as before and may carry on for quite some time. But the structural deficit that we inherited is real, substantial, and difficult. My fear is that last week's settlement adds to the structural deficit and makes the health care system that much less sustainable.

Among the many challenges that our government inherited is a collective bargaining process within the provincial public sector that makes little sense. There are far too many bargaining units for a province of this size, which leads to a never-ending bargaining process and inconsistency between bargaining units that fuels never-ending demands for "catch up" or "leap frog." It continues to puzzle me that the one critical factor that is never on the table, and that arbitrators treat as irrelevant, is the actual ability of the taxpayers to pay for the settlements. This needs to change.

In this particular case, the NSGEU picked, as its lead, the bargaining unit that would, if it went on strike, have the greatest impact on the largest number of vulnerable people. In fact, the bargaining unit was effectively on strike last week, because the Capital District Health Authority had to ramp down activity in anticipation of a walkout. In only a couple of days, hundreds or even thousands of sick Nova Scotians and their families were adversely affected. The thought process behind the union's choice disturbs me. This also needs to change.

My resignation is intended to be a wake-up call. A wake-up call not just to the government, but also to opposition members of the legislature, to the unions, and to Nova Scotians generally. Last week's settlement is a sign that we are probably not truly coming to grips with the financial sustainability of our public services, including health care.

The last time I tried some sort of wake-up call was in late 2005, when I spoke about the system of MLA expenses. What I said then was dismissed on all sides of the House. Everyone knows how that turned out.

I'm hopeful that this wake-up call, which is about a much bigger and more important issue, will have more impact. But given the state of Nova Scotia political culture, I'm not very hopeful.

The opposition should take no joy in my resignation. Let me say, as gently as I can, that their positions on questions of financial sustainability and the future of public services are simplistic, contradictory, and highly partisan. This wake-up call is for them, too.

In fact, my resignation offers Nova Scotians a useful test. Those whose inclination is to react to my resignation by attacking me or attacking the government have missed the point, and they're not the people who will move the province forward. The people who will take us forward are those who respond thoughtfully and pragmatically to the issue I'm raising.

There is only one issue today in provincial public finance, and that is sustainable funding for health care. If we get that right, then everything else will fall in place. Health takes up a larger and larger part of the budget every year. Costs for drugs, technology, doctors, other health care professionals, and utilization are very difficult to contain. Expectations and demands are high. This is not a Nova Scotia issue, and it is not a party issue. It is the same in every province, no matter which government is in power. The growth in health costs means that every year there is less and less for other important public services like education, transportation, and support for the poor and disabled. That's why the financial sustainability of health care has to be everybody's issue.

I have taken the province's finances as far as I can take them. We have done some good and necessary things to put the province's finances back on a sustainable footing. Now it's someone else's turn. I'm not concerned about who that will be because there is a tremendous amount of talent within the NDP caucus.

Let me now address some of the obvious practical questions.

I am resigning my Cabinet positions, but I am not resigning my seat in the House. It has been my privilege to represent the people of Halifax Fairview as their MLA since 2001, and I will continue to serve them in that capacity.

I will not re-offer in the next election.

I will continue to sit as a member of the NDP caucus, assuming that they will permit me to do so. There is an important distinction to be drawn between my role as a Cabinet minister and my role as a member of the caucus. As a Cabinet minister, I must support all major decisions or policy directions or resign. As a member of the caucus, the test is different. I was elected as a New Democrat, and I support this government's record and I will continue to support its legislative program. I know that this distinction will be difficult for some people to understand.

This statement is now posted on my website so that everyone, and especially the people who elected me, has the opportunity to read the whole statement. I have nothing further to add to this statement, so I will not be taking any questions or doing any interviews.

I will probably not attend the House for a few days, in order to allow things to settle down a bit, but there is work to be done and I will return to the House very shortly to carry on my work on behalf of the people of Halifax Fairview.

ACKNOWLEDGEMENTS AND FURTHER READING

A politician writing about a political career has plenty of people to acknowledge, but there were a few people who went above and beyond.

Parker Donham gave me great advice about writing in general and was kind enough to devote many hours to a meticulous edit. The book is immeasurably better because of his contribution. I didn't take all of his advice, though, and that probably explains the flaws that remain.

Stephen Kimber shared his insights about the publishing industry and the emotional arc of a book-length project. He forecast correctly how I would be feeling at different stages of the writing project, making those emotions easier to deal with when they came.

Three people—Parker, Barbara Emodi, and my wife, Tilly—read and commented on the first complete draft of the manuscript. They reassured me that I had something worth saying, and their comments were invaluable in finding the holes in the flow and the chronology.

Patrick Murphy contacted me out of the blue to see if I'd be interested in publishing with Nimbus. Patrick's interest—and the deadlines he cheerfully imposed and enforced—is why this book ever got finished. It was wonderful to have a publishing house like Nimbus behind me, and I want to thank everyone there.

The staff at the Legislative Library at Province House, led by Margaret Murphy, have been unceasingly helpful throughout my time in the legislature. Margaret, along with Anne Van Iderstine, Heather Ludlow, and David McDonald, kindly assisted with fact-checking for this book. If there are any errors of fact in this book, it's not their fault.

There aren't many books written by Nova Scotia politicians about their time in politics. There is Jeremy Akerman's *"What Have You Done For Me Lately?": A Politician Explains* (Lancelot Press, 1977) and Walter John (Jack) Hawkins's *Recollections of the Regan Years* (Lancelot Press, 1990). They're both worth reading, even many years later, for their insight about political life in Nova Scotia. Every incoming finance minister should read Janice MacKinnon's *Minding the Public Purse* (McGill-Queen's University Press, 2003). Although she was finance minister in Saskatchewan, the lessons are easily transferable. And a fine recent book that echoes many of the themes of this book, because it is based on interviews with ex-politicians, is *Tragedy in the Commons: Former Members of Parliament Speak Out About Canada's Failing Democracy* (Random House Canada, 2014). If you're thinking of getting into politics, read it.